Dakhleh Oasis Project: Monograph 8

The Dakhleh Oasis Project: Preliminary Reports on the 1992--1993 and 1993–1994 Field Seasons

Dakhleh Oasis Project:
Preliminary Reports on the 1992–1993
and 1993–1994 Field Seasons

Edited by C. A. Hope and A. J. Mills

with contributions by

M. Birrell, G. E. Bowen, I. Gardner, C. A. Hope, O. E. Kaper, C. Marchini,
M. M. A. McDonald, J. McKenzie, A. J. Mills, S. F. Patten, U. Thanheiser,
K. Walker and H. Whitehouse

Oxbow Books

Oxford and Oakville

Published by
Oxbow Books, Park End Place, Oxford OX1 1HN

ISBN 1 900188 95 3

This book is available direct from
Oxbow Books, Park End Place, Oxford OX1 1HN
(Phone: 01865-241249; Fax: 01865-794449)

and

The David Brown Book Company
PO Box 511, Oakville, CT 06779, USA
(Phone: 860-945-9329; Fax 860-945-9468)

and

from our website

www.oxbowbooks.com

*Front Cover: Painted panel of Isis from the Main Temple
at Ismant el-Kharab*

*Printed in Great Britain at
The Short Run Press, Exeter*

Editors' Preface

The publication of the preliminary reports on the work conducted by the Dakhleh Oasis Project during its 1992–1994 field seasons which appear in this volume has been delayed unavoidably since their preparation between 1993 and 1995. The editors would like to thank all of the contributors for their patience and co-operation both in relation to this delay and in assisting with its final appearance. The text of each contribution remains substantially in its original form with only minor revision, and only when it was deemed essential has reference to publications which have appeared since 1995 been inserted either by the author/s or editors. Each paper, therefore, represents the ideas of its author/s as they stood at the time of writing; in some cases these have been superceded as a result of more recent research. Thus, in presenting some of the papers herein they document a previous stage in the development of our understanding of certain issues which we hope will, nevertheless, be informative. The bibliographic details for the references cited in each contribution are presented together at the end of the volume.

Initial editing of the contributions by Mary McDonald, Anthony Mills and Karen Walker was undertaken by Anthony Mills, and of those dealing with work at Ismant el-Kharab by Colin Hope. Some further editing on all contributions was then carried out by Anthony Mills in the period up to 1997 and in 1998 this was undertaken again by Colin Hope. During the latter process much assistance was received from Gillian Bowen and Bruce Parr.

Contents

Preliminary Reports on the Work During the 1992–1993 and 1993–1994 Field Seasons

Anthony J. Mills

The 1992–1993 Season

The 1992–1993 field season of the Dakhleh Oasis Project began on 5 November 1992 with the arrival in Cairo of the director and Mr Zielinski. The expedition camp was established at Ezbet Bashendi by 12 November and a satellite camp was also set up at Maohoub, specifically for the work at Deir el-Haggar. The work continued without interruption until 31 March 1993, when the camp was closed for the summer.

The project was sponsored this season by the Society for the Study of Egyptian Antiquities and the Royal Ontario Museum, both of which subscribed funds to the expedition, the American Research Centre in Egypt and The University of Durham. Additional funding was provided from the Australian Research Council to Dr Hope, the Natural Sciences and Engineering Research Council of Canada operating grant to Professor Churcher, the Canadian International Development Agency, The Bioanthropology Foundation, The Society of Antiquaries of London, The Manchester Museum, Egyptair, Benjamin Film Laboratories Ltd., the General Packaging Company Ltd., C. Baines, S. Carter, G. Carter, R. and E. Cromby, J. G. Lipscombe and from the institutional support of various individual members of the project. To all of these the project is most grateful for their generosity.

The staff of this season's expedition consisted of the following members: A. Alcock, papyrologist; M. Berry, Museum of Victoria, conservator; M. Birrell, Macquarie University, archaeologist; G. E. Bowen, Monash University, archaeologist and numismatist; M. E. Bowman, Monash University, archaeologist; E. C. Brock, Canadian Institute in Egypt, archaeologist; L. Pinch Brock, artist; C. S. Churcher, University of Toronto, archaeozoologist; W. B. Churcher, photographer; R. Colvin, photographer; M. Cook, Henry Ford Hospital, physical anthropologist; J. A. M. Davies, University of Toronto, archaeologist; I. Gardner, Edith Cowan University, papyrologist; A. F. Hollett, Royal Ontario Museum, photographer and technician; C. A. Hope, Monash University/The Museum of Victoria, archaeologist; O. E. Kaper, Netherlands Institute for Archaeology and Arabic Studies, epigrapher; J. E. Knudstad, architect; K. Kroeper, The Egyptian Museum, Berlin, petroglyphs recorder; L. Krzyzaniak, The Archaeological Museum, Poznan, petroglyphs recorder; D. LeBaron, conservator; C. A. Marlow, University of Durham, physical anthropologist; M. M. A. McDonald, University of Calgary, archaeologist; A. J. Mills, director; L. F. Mills, archaeologist; J. E. Molto, Lakehead University, physical anthropologist; J. P. O'Carroll, artist; B. E. Parr, artist; S. F. Patten, Macquarie University, ceramicist; P. G. Sheldrick, Society for the Study of Egyptian Antiquities, physical anthropologist; U. Thanheiser, University of Vienna, bioarchaeologist; K. Walker, University of Toronto, archaeologist; J. Walter, University of Vienna, botanist; M. F. Wiseman, University of Toronto, archaeologist; K. A. Worp, University of Amsterdam, papyrologist; A. K. Zielinski, conservator; B. Zimmerman, physical anthropologist; M. Zimmerman, University of Pennsylvania, physical anthropologist.

As always, a great number of colleagues and friends in Egypt must be thanked for their kindness and encouragement. Within the Egyptian Antiquities Organization, The President, Professor Mohammed Ibrahim Bakr, Mr Mutawa Balboush and Mr Kemal Fahmy at Abbasiyeh, Mr Adel Hussein and his staff in the New Valley, and the two representatives who accompanied the expedition, Mr Ashraf el-Tarabishi and Mr Maher Bashendi were all extremely helpful to the project. Again, Mr Senaid Safina, a conservator from the New Valley, joined the work at Deir el-Haggar to great advantage. Dr Farouk el-Tellawi, the Governor of the New Valley and Mr Mohammed Abdel Mohmen of the Dakhleh Council were of considerable help to us. Finally, we are most grateful to Mr E. C. Brock and Mr Saad B. Mohammed of the Canadian Institute in Egypt who made the administration and logistics of the season much simpler for us.

What follows is a short account of the season's activities, while more extensive reporting on Holocene

Prehistory, 'Ein Birbiyeh, Deir el-Haggar, and the work at Ismant el-Kharab will be found below. Site locations are identified on the map, Figure 1.

Environmental Studies

The analysis of soils and debris by Dr Thanheiser begins to yield preliminary results. Screening has resulted in the collection of considerable charcoal and two 'grass seeds' from the Bashendi Cultural Unit hut circle excavations. This is the first recovered mid-Holocene floral material from Dakhleh and will be of extreme importance for considerations of the economy and for landscape reconstruction for the period. The plant remains at Ismant el-Kharab also yield a large variety of species, including field crops, garden crops, and of various flowers. Faunal identifications at both of these sites have become more specific with the excavation of materials that are less broken up. Professor Churcher reports gazelle, several sizes of birds, a goat-sized animal, a small bovid or hartebeest from the mid-Holocene hut circle site and suggests extensive hunting of gazelle and birds, which would provide a reason for the numbers of fine arrow-points found on Bashendi Cultural Unit sites. From Ismant el-Kharab, we see pig, goat and chicken as the predominant domesticates. In particular, pigs were slaughtered as young animals, while other species were eaten at an older age due, presumably, to their being able to provide other commodities like milk and eggs to the economy. Other meat sources were pigeon, cow and camel. An interesting find this season was bones of a Nile catfish, presumably dried or salted and traded out to the oasis.

Archaeological Studies

Dr. Wiseman probed deeper into the unresolved issue of a late Pleistocene (~20,000 years bp) presence in the oasis. The collection and analysis of chipped stone materials from locations south of Sheikh Muftah, around the edges of an ancient basin, strongly suggest an identification with the Khargan originally described by Caton-Thompson (1952, 29–30) in her work in the Kharga Oasis. Dating of this 'Khargan' is still problematic for, while Caton-Thompson places it earlier than the Aterian, a single date from Dungul Oasis indicates a time between 20,000 and 30,000 years bp (Hobler and Hester 1969, 14, Table 2). If the dating can be sustained, the earlier part of the late Pleistocene may have both a prototypical collection and a locality in the Dakhleh Oasis. Dr. McDonald (McDonald and Walker, herein) spent the season excavating and mapping at Locality 270 (30/450–F10–2), the large group of hut circles dating to the Bashendi Cultural Unit, some 7,000 years bp. This site, the largest known from anywhere in north-east Africa, is being mapped at various scales, and excavations made to recover artefactual and economic materials. The picture emerging is one of special activity areas in parts of the site, involving extensive use of fires and grinding. It also seems clear that the site was occupied for a considerable period of time.

The village at Ismant el-Kharab (31/420–D6–1), ancient Kellis, is one of our major excavation sites and has proven to be highly productive of artefacts and materials relating to the daily and religious life during the first few centuries of our era in this isolated region (see reports, herein). This season saw further exposures in the decorated, mud-brick Shrine I, which adjoins the Main Temple. The first of Kellis' purpose-built churches was also excavated, as were two nearby peristyle tombs. East of the temple enclosure, excavation began in House 4. This, like others at the site, is well preserved, standing into the second storey, but as the result of somewhat poor construction, proved to be rather dangerous in the lower floors. A number of texts, in Greek and in Coptic and on papyrus and writing boards, were also recovered and all dating to the 4th century. Below the ground floors, a deposit of early Roman period material was discovered.

Excavation also continued (Birrell, herein) at the cemeteries associated with Ismant el-Kharab (31/420–C5–1 and 31/420–C5–2). The total of 42 inhumations has so far been recovered and are of interest for a variety of factors to both the physical anthropologists and the archaeologists. The first cemetery appears to be of a different date than the second. The one has cave tombs with multiple burials, some mummified bodies, and a few cases of burial within cartonnage, some of which has been made utilizing papyrus on which is demotic Egyptian writing. The other has simple pit graves with single burials which are skeletonized. Neither cemetery has many grave nor offering goods, in the case of 31/420–C5–1 primarily due to plundering. One burial displays symptoms of leprosy.

Work at the sandstone temple of Amun-Nakht at 'Ein Birbiyeh (31/435–K5–1; Mills, herein) has chiefly been concentrated in the gateway in past seasons. This has now been re-filled with clean sand to give it a long-term protection. This season our attention has turned to the façade of the temple building and the 'Porch', the room lying directly behind it. The excavation proved quite fruitful and, although the building is in rather worse condition than the gateway, good new information has been obtained.

At Deir el-Haggar (33/390–F9–1), where we began a joint project of rehabilitation with the Egyptian Antiquities Organization last season, there was a continuation of this work (Mills, herein). The entire temple has now been cleared of sand and fallen stone debris and the reconstruction of the north wall of the Hypostyle Hall begun. In addition, all the ceiling slabs and fragments, originally removed by Remelé in 1875, have now been recovered and will be reassembled in a display area within the temenos area.

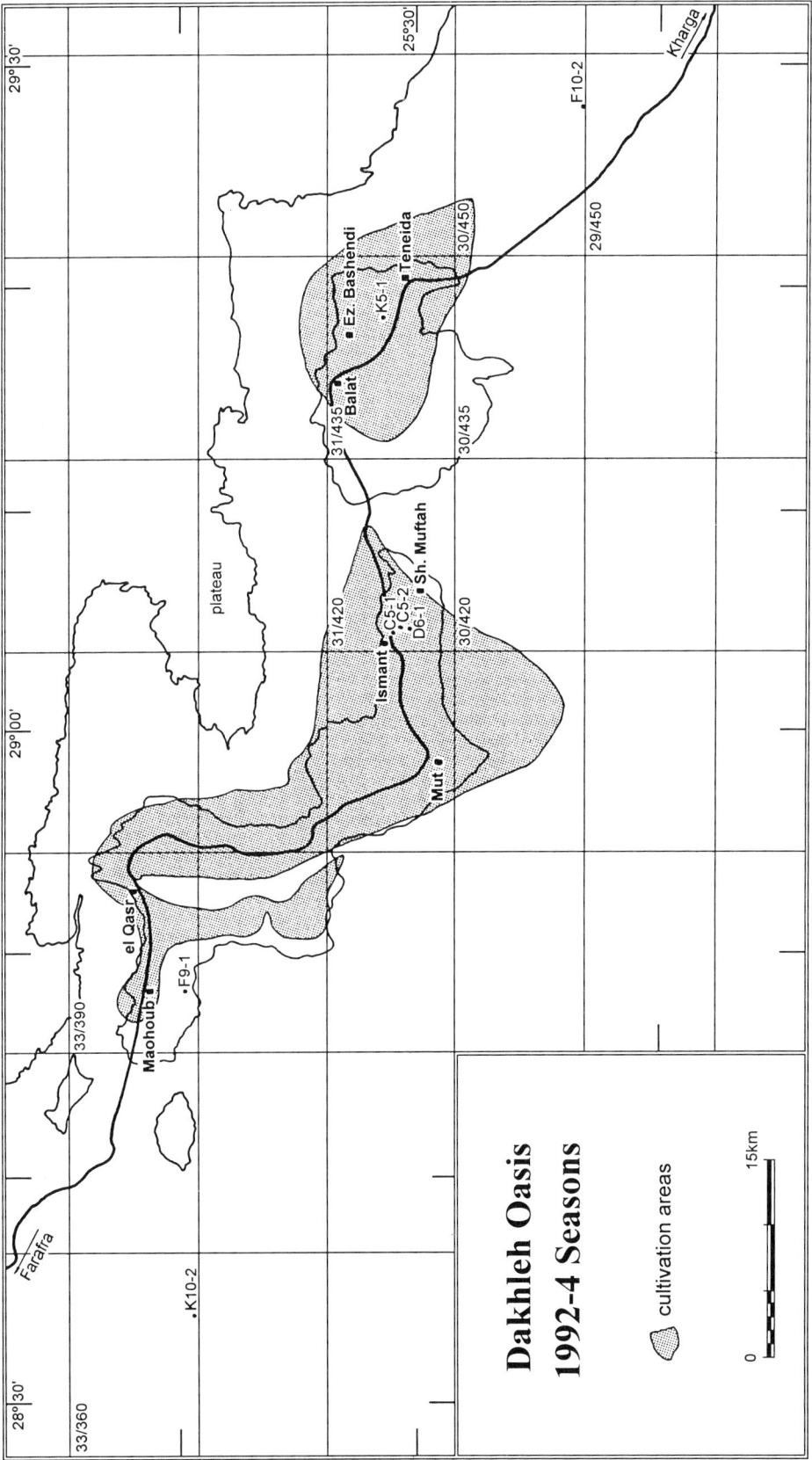

Figure 1 Dakhleh Oasis: locations of the sites referred to in the text.

The 1993–1994 Season

The 1993–1994 field season began on 13 November 1993 with the arrival in Cairo of the director and Mr Zielinski. The field camp was set up at Ezbet Bashendi, in our usual headquarters in eastern Dakhleh, and a satellite camp also established at Maohoub for the work at Deir el-Haggar. Field work continued without interruption until 28 February 1994 when the camps were closed.

The work of the project was sponsored this season by the Royal Ontario Museum, the Society for the Study of Egyptian Antiquities, both of which subscribed funds to the project, The American Research Centre in Egypt and The University of Durham. Additional funding was provided from the Egyptology Society of Victoria to Dr Hope, the Natural Sciences and Engineering Research Council of Canada operating grant to Professor Churcher, The Bioanthropology Foundation, The Leverhulme Trust, The Manchester Museum, Egyptair, the General Packaging Company Ltd, C. Baines, S. Carter, G. Carter, R. and E. Cromby, J. G. Lipscombe, M. Loftmark, P. I. W. Mayne, B. Partridge, A. F. Shore, M. Wheat, and from the institutional support of various individual members of the project. To all of these, the Dakhleh Oasis Project is most grateful.

The staff of this season's expedition comprised the following members: A. Alcock, papyrologist; B. Allardice, University of Melbourne, technician; A. Aufterheide, University of Minnesota, physical anthropologist; M. Berry, Museum of Victoria, conservator; M. Birrell, Macquarie University, archaeologist; G. E. Bowen, Monash University, archaeologist and numismatist; E. C. Brock, Canadian Institute in Egypt, archaeologist; L. Cartmell, Valley View Regional Hospital, physical anthropologist; C. S. Churcher, University of Toronto, archaeozoologist; A. Dunsmore, Monash University, ceramicist; I. Gardner, Edith Cowan University, papyrologist; A. Glaser, University of Vienna, physicist; C. A. Hope, Monash University/The Museum of Victoria, archaeologist; O. E. Kaper, Netherlands Institute for Archaeology and Arabic Studies, epigrapher; J. E. Knudstad, architect; C. Marchini, University of Pisa, archaeologist; M. M. A. McDonald, University of Calgary, archaeologist; A. J. Mills, director; L. F. Mills, archaeologist; J. E. Molto, Lakehead University, physical anthropologist; S. I. Fairgrieve, Laurentian University, physical anthropologist; J. P. O'Carroll, artist; S. F. Patten, Macquarie University, ceramicist; R. L. Shaw, Royal Ontario Museum, designer; P. G. Sheldrick, Society for the Study of Egyptian Antiquities, physical anthropologist; U. Thanheiser, University of Vienna, bioarchaeologist; K. A. Worp, University of Amsterdam, papyrologist; A. K. Zielinski, conservator; M. Zlonis, University of Minnesota, physical anthropologist.

Finally, we are always grateful to our colleagues and friends in Egypt, and wish to thank them for all their support and assistance. Within the Egyptian Antiquities Organization, Dr Abdel Halim Nur el Din, Mohandes Ahmed Gabr, Mr Mutawa Balboush and Mr Kemal Fahmy at Abbasiyeh, Mr Adel Hussein and his staff in the New Valley, and the representatives, Mr Sayed Yamani and Mr Ashraf el-Tarabishi, who accompanied the expedition. Mr Senaid Safina, a conservator, joined the work at Deir el-Haggar as last season. The governor of the New Valley, General Mohammed Ezzat el-Sayed, was particularly helpful in providing equipment for Deir el-Haggar, and our old friend, Mohammed Abdel Mohmen of the Dakhleh Oasis Council was most generous with his time. In Cairo, our logistical and administrative support was provided by the director, Mr E. C. Brock, and his assistant, Mr Saad B. Mohammed, of the Canadian Institute in Egypt.

What follows now is an outline of the work done in the oasis by the project during this season, while fuller accounts of the Holocene Prehistory research, work at the temples of 'Ein Birbiyeh and Deir el-Haggar, and of the work at Ismant el-Kharab, by various members of that team, are provided.

Environmental Studies

In 1993–1994, Professor Churcher was able to identify the presence of caprovine from Bashendi Cultural Unit levels at Sheikh Muftah and, at Bir Talata el-Maohoub, of hippopotamus. Additionally, a pendant made from a valve of a lamellibranch, and the jaw of a large gazelle were identified at the latter site (32/390–D2–2). At Ismant el-Kharab (31/420–D6–1), the animals identified were pig (*Sus*), goat/sheep (*Capra/Ovis*), chicken (*Gallus*), cow (*Bos*), ass (*Equus*) and pigeon (*Columba*). In addition to these usual fauna, goose (*Anser*) or duck (*Anas*), Dorcas gazelle (*Gazella dorcas*) and some small birds were observed. There was evidence of butchering on a donkey.

Dr Thanheiser was, in 1993–1994, accompanied by Dr A. Glaser, a physicist from the Institute for Botany, Vienna University. Together, they have developed a new flotation device, which works by electrostatically separating charcoal from the soil matrix. This is a major advance for flotation in the dry conditions of the Dakhleh region. The usual dry flotation is a slow and very dusty method, while wet flotation is impractical because the charcoal disintegrates in the water. This season Dr Thanheiser succeeded in isolating all the charred plant remains from the past three seasons' excavations at early Holocene sites.

Archaeological Studies

The Pleistocene prehistorian, Dr Wiseman, continued her research into the question of human habitation in the Western Desert in the late Pleistocene, ~60,000 to 11,000 bp. With the initial analysis of collected artefactual materials indicating a connection with the 'Khargan' industry described by Caton-Thompson and mounting evidence that the Khargan post-dates the Aterian at Kharga, indications are that there was no complete depopulation of the Dakhleh Oasis area at this hyperarid time. The work of the Holocene prehistorian (McDonald, herein) was again concentrated at Locality 270 (30/450–F10–2). Mapping of structures in one area, with excavation of a large pit structure were the main activities and have added considerable detail to our understanding of the Bashendi Cultural Unit occupation of the oasis.

At Ismant el-Kharab (31/420–D6–1) there were excavations within the Main Temple of Tutu, to examine the floor deposits (Whitehouse and Hope, herein). In addition, there were a number of particular studies of human remains, glass, plaster and stone sculpture, ceramics, coins and epigraphic and papyrological recording of scenes and texts.

Work continued at the Temple of Deir el-Haggar (33/390–F10–1) for the third season. This joint Dakhleh Oasis Project / Egyptian Antiquities Organization venture resulted in the restoration of the north wall of the Hypostyle Hall and the west end, the installation of a protective ceiling in the Sanctuary, the Processional Way brick columns and the mud-brick temenos wall have been capped for protection, and various wooden constructions introduced into doorways.

Holocene Prehistory: Interim Report
on the 1992 Season

Mary M. A. McDonald and Karen Walker

Our 1992 season ran for just over two months until 13 March. The focus this season was mostly on one large site in south-eastern Dakhleh, Locality 270. This site, which consists of numerous stone rings, putative hut foundations, was mapped and portions of it excavated. We were assisted in the mapping by P. G. Sheldrick, while J. O'Carroll drew the artefacts and A. J. Mills photographed them. Animal bones were analysed by C. S. Churcher and floral remains by U. Thanheiser. We benefited, in addition, from the collaboration and material assistance offered by A. J. Mills, C. S. Churcher, M. R. Kleindienst, L. Krzyzaniak and K. Kroeper. Finally, one of us (McDonald) was supported in the 1992 season by an SSHRC Canada Research Fellowship (award #455–88–0023), held in the Department of Archaeology, University of Calgary.

Locality 270: Introduction

Locality 270 (30/450–F10–2) was discovered in 1990 by I. A. Brookes, L. Krzyzaniak and K. Kroeper (McDonald 1990b). It is located just to the east of the South-East Basin (McDonald 1990a), upon a bedrock interfluve within the wadi system that originates atop the plateau to the north-east. Locality 270, which associated artefacts suggest is a mid-Holocene or Bashendi Cultural Unit site, consists of an estimated (in 1990) 150 stone circles. This would make it by far the largest site reported anywhere in the eastern Sahara for the Mid-Holocene.

In our 1992 work we had several general goals:

1) to produce a site map, in the process obtaining an accurate count of the stone features;
2) to study construction of the structures;
3) to investigate the history of the site, addressing such issues as contemporaneity of structures, possible re-occupation, length and season(s) of occupation, and so on; and
4) to address the issue of adaptation, through a study of artefacts and economic data.

Locality 270 is a sprawling site occupying a V-shaped valley within the sandstone interfluve; structures are scattered for about 200 m along one arm of the valley, and 300 m along the other. In 1992 a skeleton map of the site was produced using a theodolite to plot in hut circles and other features, and the outlines of ridges and hills (Figure 1). Generally, a single reading was taken from the centre of each round structure and two, one at each end, for elongated forms. In addition, east-west lines were shot across Locality 270 to give us two cross-sections of the site.

The original estimate of 150 stone circles proves too low. There are 200 apparent structures on the site, plus other features such as stone clusters, small bin-like forms and what appear to be activity areas, littered with grinding equipment and other artefacts. Most of the structures are roughly circular, bilobed, or crescent-shaped, often measuring three to five metres across; nearly one third of the total, however, are rectangular-shaped, running up to 12 m in length. With few exceptions, structures are confined to the valley floor, where they are distributed, with some clustering evident, on land lying between one and two metres below site datum. A slightly deeper area, a 100 metre-long basin along the east branch of the valley, is almost bare of circles.

Excavation at Locality 270

Questions concerning site history and site economy were addressed through the detailed mapping and excavation of individual structures. In preparation, two grids, each enclosing several stone features, were established: Grid A, 30 (east-west) by 18 m, in the west arm of the site, and Grid B, 20 by 24 m in the east, later expanded by 24 m² in its south-east corner (Figure 1). Within Grid A, four features, labelled Huts (H) 1 through 4, were mapped and excavated, while in B, two, H-173 and H-174, were studied initially. The four Grid A huts (Figure 2) are all

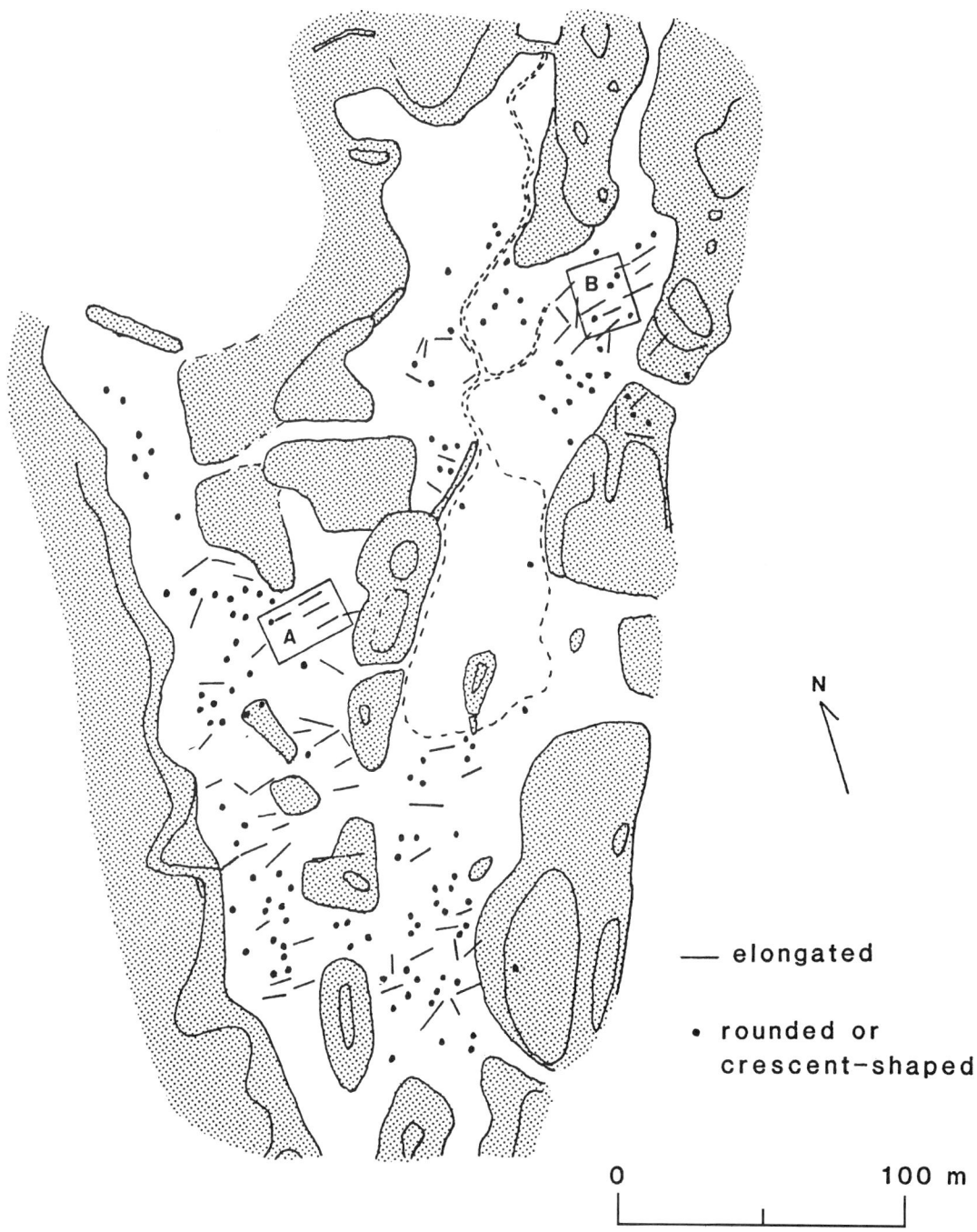

N

—— elongated

• rounded or
   crescent-shaped

0   100 m

Figure 1 Locality 270: location of structures and Grids A and B.

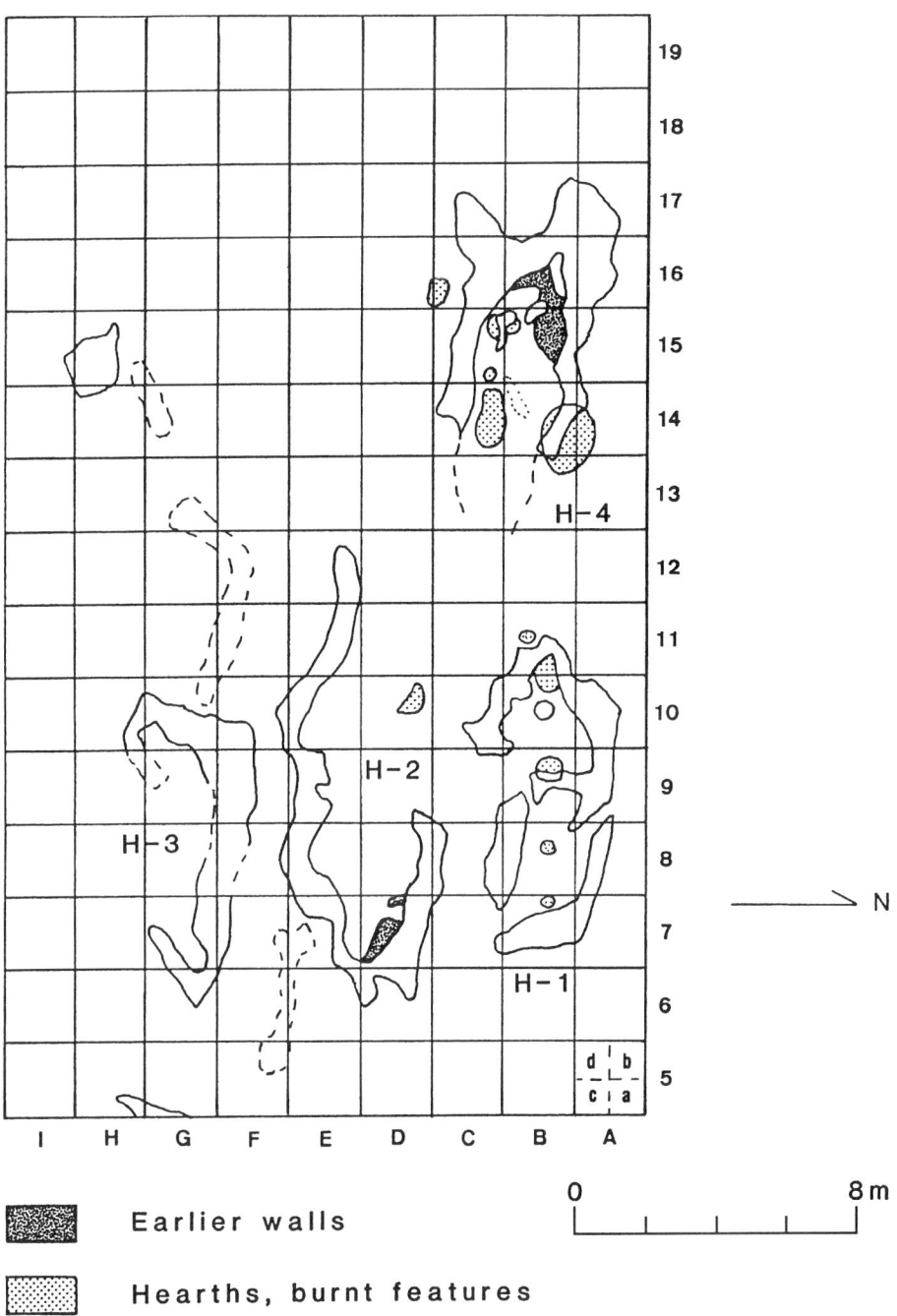

Figure 2 *Locality 270: Grid A.*

elongated structures oriented east-west, although H-1 could actually be classified as bilobed, while H-4, to the west of the other three, has a crescent-shaped unit tacked on its west end. Of the Grid B features, H-174 is crescent-shaped, while H-173 is roughly circular (Figure 3). The two grided areas differ in certain respects: compared with B, the Grid A location is much more deflated and with fewer artefacts on the surface, but the stone walls of its features are generally better preserved.

Construction techniques in both areas are similar. The structures consist of slabs of the local sandstone or ironstone. In contrast to the pattern in the early Holocene Masara C Cultural Unit stone circles in this area, where most slabs are set upright (McDonald 1991; 1990b), at Locality 270 stones are, with some exceptions, laid down flat, usually two or more courses deep. Generally, the bottom tier consists of large rocks measuring up to 40–50 cm in length, with smaller ones placed over them, although in parts of H-174, the pattern is reversed, with the large stones on top. Throughout the site, gaps in hut walls suggest one (abandoned?) structure may have been robbed of stones to build another.

Aside from these unpatterned gaps, walls are not uniform throughout individual structures. In all of the excavated four-sided features, the north wall, and often particularly its north-west corner, is higher, wider, and more continuous than the other walls. Likewise, in the crescent-shaped H-174, the apogee is to the north-west.

Evidence concerning the treatment of walls and on the nature of any superstructure is scanty, given the generally deflated nature of the deposit. Most walls in fact seem to be of dry-stone construction, the slabs stacked on bedrock or some other surface, and now partly buried by aeolian sand. The deposit in parts of H-1, 4, 173 and 174, however, is different; it is fairly consolidated, with a high silt content, sometimes salty, and breaks into polygonal-sided lumps. The presence of organics in the lumps, at least in H-4 and 173, suggests a possible anthropogenic origin. In H-1, 4 and 173, the lumpy deposit seems centred on the north wall where it occurs between and under rocks. Outside H-173, pockets of it are found, just north of the wall, while in H-1 and 4, it extends across much of the hut floor. In H-1, two small hearths are dug through the material to bedrock, while in H-4, a ridge of it forms a partial curb for a hearth. The deposit may therefore have served as a building material, being packed, for instance, as a filler around wall rocks.

There is still little evidence concerning the nature of any superstructure for the huts. The wall slabs laid flat might suggest tent footings, although the variable heights of existing walls and the fact that stones are still stacked several tiers deep in places, might argue against this function. Any tent covering would have to be of animal skin, unless caprines were already present to supply goat hair (see below). Likewise, there is little direct evidence for the use of reeds or wickerwork in a superstructure. None of the mud lumps within the structures bore impressions of such materials, although several tiny (< 2 cm²) mud fragments from a feature west of H-173, excavated in 1993, bore reed or mat impressions. Very few post moulds were encountered in these structures. Two quite large ones, up to 15–20 cm across, appeared in the north-west corner of H-173, and two others, 8–10 cm in diameter, outside to the west of the hut, but they form no discernible pattern.

As for the interiors of the features, those excavated in 1992 do not appear to be semi-subterranean or pit structures, such as the earlier Masara C Unit dwellings in Dakhleh or those on Predynastic Period settlements in the Nile Valley (McDonald 1990b; Hassan 1988). Within Locality 270 structures, people built and then lived on the existing surface, although in parts of three huts, 1, 3 and 4, the walls are built upon ridges in the bedrock, thus enclosing shallow natural hollows.

Some structures contain more features than others. As mentioned above, two hearths, marked by charcoal, ash, and red-stained soil and stones, are dug through the lumpy deposit in the western half of H-1. A third pit in this area, 45 cm across and lined with small cobbles, shows no sign of burning. Two additional ashy patches occur in the more deflated sandy deposit of the eastern end of the hut. Hut 4 features a fairly elaborate hearth towards its eastern end, set within one of the bedrock hollows mentioned above, and further protected to the north-west by a rim of the lumpy material. Two other ash-filled hollows to the west of the first underlie the lumpy deposit. The crescent on the western end of H-4 was bisected and the southern half dug to bedrock; here, no features were found. Likewise, there was little evidence of features in either Huts 2 or 3, both quite deflated, although one small ashy patch was noted in the north-west (open) corner of H-2. Other possible outside hearths include a feature in a small alcove just south of the western end of H-1, and another in a similarly sheltered spot just beyond the south-west corner of H-4. In Grid B, the floor of H-173 is uniformly an unconsolidated deposit with traces of burning everywhere, but no well-defined hearths. Just to the east, charcoal fragments are commonly found in and around the crescent-shaped H-174, while one red-stained patch within the arc yields some charcoal and is bounded by a few small rocks.

Evidence Bearing on Site Life-History

Despite the generally shallow and fragmentary nature of the deposit, there is considerable evidence from each excavated structure in both of the grided areas to suggest that Locality 270 witnessed more than a single occupation. Individual structures provide evidence of phasing and re-occupation during their life histories, while over time there are changes in the location of structures and perhaps even site function.

All excavated structures, except apparently H-173, underwent changes over time. In H-4, as mentioned above, a pair of ash-filled features and the surface associated with them are covered by a consolidated layer, itself overlain by a row of large rocks sitting on the present surface (Figure 2). The large hearth towards the eastern end of the hut seems to pertain to this later phase, as does a change – an expansion to the north-west – in the western wall of the structure. The crescent-shaped feature at the western end of the hut may also have been built at this time. As for H-1, the north-south curtain wall that bisects the structure seems to be a late addition; it overlies a hearth that was dug into the consolidated layer in the middle of the hut.

Changes in the other huts seem to point to the occasional abandonment and re-occupation of these features. Thus in H-2, a pocket of laminated silts contained within the wall of the low-lying eastern alcove may represent a flooding episode early in the life of the hut. Subsequently, an additional layer of stones was placed on the hut wall in this area, but the upper layer is slightly out of alignment with the lower, and its rocks sit atop, or wedged into, a layer of sand that itself lies over the silts (Figure 4a). Both the shift in wall location and the build-up of deposit between the

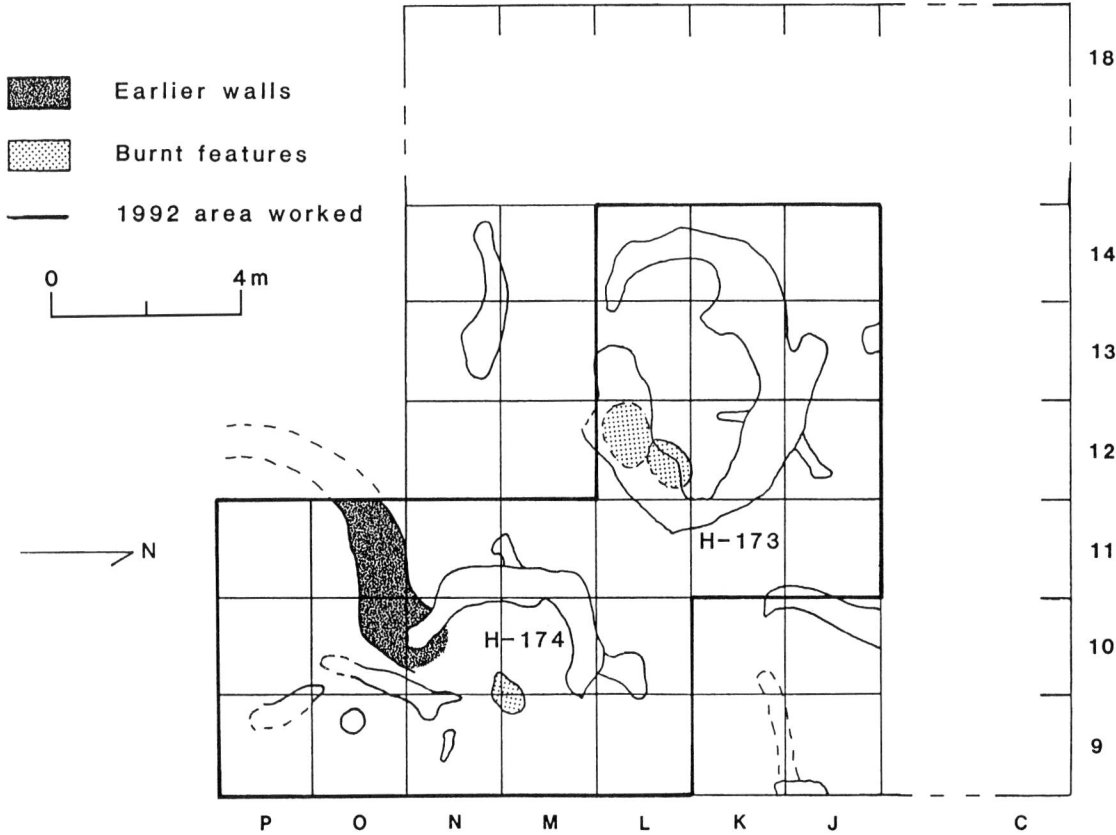

Figure 3 Locality 270: Grid B south-east corner.

two phases suggests the structure may have been abandoned for a period. A similar hiatus can be postulated for H-3, the north wall of which shows the same pattern of a sandy layer between lower and upper courses of rock.

A more complex picture of site history emerges from the south-east corner of Grid B, where there is evidence for at least two generations of huts (Figure 3). One end of the surface feature, H-174, overlaps a large lower wall, 3.4+ by 1.4 m in its excavated portion, that curves off to the west-south-west. A layer, 5 cm thick, of compacted sand between the lower and upper walls at the overlap of the two structures suggests an interval between the abandonment of the earlier and the building of the later feature. Similar evidence, the build-up of deposit between courses of rock, suggests breaks in the occupation of both the earlier and later structures themselves: one break for the early and perhaps two for the later structure. Other fragments of walls found to the south-east of H-174 seem to be contemporaneous with this later structure.

Other surface structures seem to be built over a different sort of deposit. The wall stones of H-173 sit well above sterile soil, upon 30 cm of fairly loose, possibly midden, deposit containing the occasional charcoal fragment, pocket of ash, artefact or bone scrap. Near the top of this deposit, but on a surface below the level of the H-173 west wall (Figure 4b), is a patch 40 cm across consisting of ash and charcoal, and underlain by a layer of sand

stained a deep red. Similar, even more prominent, burnt features occur under the southern wall of H-173, lying 10+ cm below the wall rocks. One of them, in the southwest quadrant of square L12, is a black-stained, slightly concave surface, 1.4 by 1 m, with charcoal scatters, red patches and a few small rocks. A second such feature lies just to the north-east at a slightly higher level. An apparently analogous phenomenon is found in H-4 of Grid A, where a similar charcoal-strewn feature underlies both the stones of the north-west corner of the structure, and two layers of consolidated deposit that lie immediately under the stones. In H-3, a portion of the north wall lies, not on one of these hearth-like features *per se*, but on a surface strewn with charcoal, suggesting that such a feature lay nearby when the hut was built.

All of these burnt features underlying (predating?) the Locality 270 stone-built structures, might be akin to a more extensive similar feature lying west of H-173, which was investigated in 1993. While the pattern is still quite fragmentary, it is possible that these distinctive 'burnt features', found in both grided areas, some yielding a similar range of artefacts, and none, so far, directly associated with stone structures, might represent a set of activities or type of occupation early in the site, different from that associated with the structures currently found on the surface of the site.

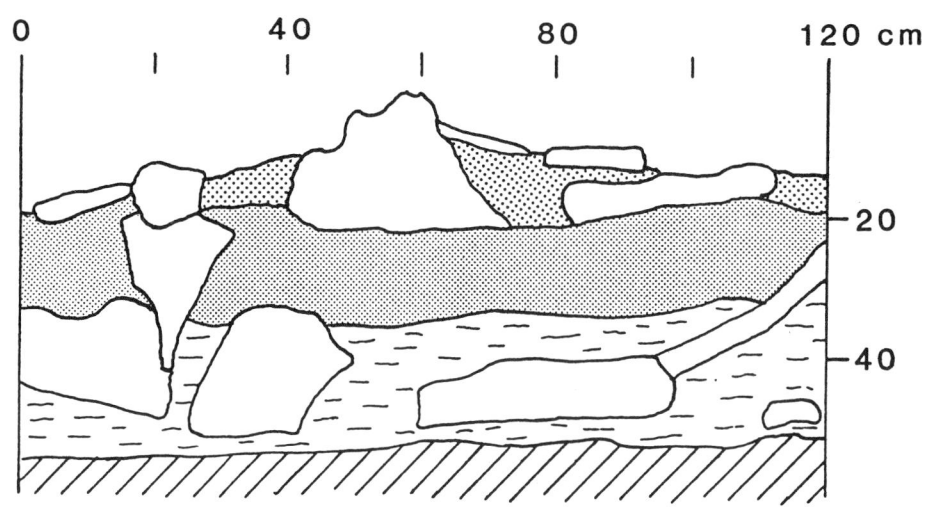

a: Grid A, H-2, D7d-c, c. north balk

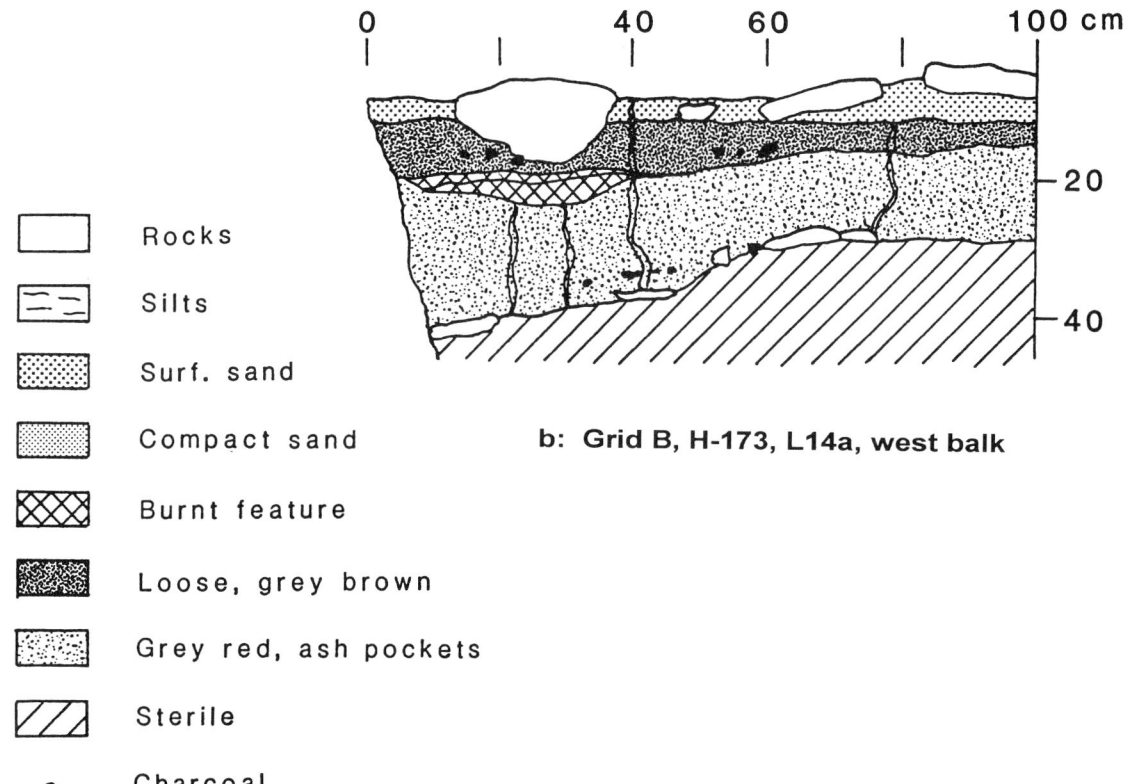

Rocks

Silts

Surf. sand

Compact sand   **b: Grid B, H-173, L14a, west balk**

Burnt feature

Loose, grey brown

Grey red, ash pockets

Sterile

Charcoal

Figure 4 Locality 270: sections through Grid A H-2 and Grid B H-173.

Site Economy and Dating

Information on the economy at Locality 270 is still somewhat scanty. In 1992, a total of 17 soil samples were collected for archaeobotanical analysis from various contexts within both grids. While no detailed results are available yet, preliminary reports indicate that plant macrofossils (grass seeds) were preserved in at least some of these contexts.

Generally, animal bones are not well preserved, particularly in Grid A. The small, usually fragile remains from 1992 include two sizes of bird (chicken-size and smaller), dorcas gazelle, and another bovid the size of sheep/goat or a larger gazelle. Two fragments of a cowrie shell, possibly from the Red Sea, were found on Grid B. On present evidence, it cannot be determined if any of the animals were domesticated.

A total of 1405 pieces of chipped stone from the 1992 season have been analysed; the material from around Huts 2 and 3 in Grid A has not yet been studied. Distribution is much denser in Grid B than A; the area around H-173 yielded 15.8 lithics per m², that around H-4, 1.2 per m². The total includes 70 formal tools, plus 8 cores, and 3 hammerstones or abraders. Of the tools, 25% are piercers, 25% retouched pieces and 17% arrowheads. There are also small quantities of, in descending order, denticulates (7%), notches, knives, microliths, burins, combination tools, drills and scrapers. Roughly the same range of tools is found in Grids A and B, except that the small collection from A includes no retouched pieces. The bulk of the tools come from outside rather than within structures, although higher than expected proportions of denticulates and arrowheads are found within huts. Two of the four knives come from inside structures, and the presence of resharpening flakes with a knife in H-1 attest its use in that context.

Other categories of artefacts found on Locality 270 include ostrich-eggshell beads, grinding stones, a few small sherds and labrets and smaller items fashioned in calcite. Of the 135 ostrich-eggshell beads in the mapped areas, excluding those around Huts 2 and 3, fully 96% came from Grid B. Both grinding slabs and handstones are found on 270, but the only ones from the mapped

areas were four small fragments around H-173. Two of these came from the vicinity of the burnt feature under the south wall, which also yielded a few used flakes and some ostrich-eggshell beads. The only ceramics noted were a few small Bashendi Cultural Unit sherds in the vicinity of Grid B (Hope 1998). None were recovered from mapped or excavated contexts.

The 270 assemblage as a whole – chipped stone types, numerous ostrich eggshell beads, scarcity of pottery, presence of calcite items and the faunal list – suggests the (earlier) Bashendi A Cultural Unit, rather than Bashendi B Cultural Unit (McDonald, 1990c). A suite of seven radiocarbon dates, ranging from 7340 to 6470 bp and averaging 6867 bp, seems to put the occupation at the end of the Bashendi A sequence (Table 1). This list of dates, however, ranging over 1,000 years if the standard deviations of the earliest and latest is considered, is too blunt a tool for addressing questions concerning the contemporaneity of various portions of, or structures within, the site.

Discussion

Although the study of Locality 270 is in its preliminary stages, we can begin to address the question posed in the introduction concerning site history and adaptations. One point to emerge is that 270 is not simply a short-term, single occupation site. The evidence for alterations within huts – more than one generation of hearths in H-4, the late addition of a curtain wall in H-1 – suggests that structures were occupied over some period of time. On the other hand, various lines of evidence, most notably the widespread stratigraphic evidence for periodic abandonment, indicate this was not a permanent, year-round habitation site. The relative scarcity of cultural debris suggests this too, as does ethnographic evidence from sites world-wide with similar insubstantial architecture (Gilman 1987).

If the site was occupied regularly in a particular season, then the structures themselves suggest that season was winter. The clear emphasis on a strong north wall, where the several courses of stone may have been reinforced by

Table 1 Radiocarbon dates from Locality 270. No dates calibrated. Ostrich-eggshell (OES) dates adjusted for isotopic fractionation by adding a constant factor of 350 years.

Lab. No.	Material, Context	Age bp	Adjusted Age bp
Gd-4844	CH, Grid A, H-1 W hearth, B11a	N.A.	
Gd-6636	CH, Grid A, H-1 Hearth under curtain wall, B9c–d	6860±80	
Gd-6637	CH, Grid A, H-4 Hearth under lumpy, C15a–b	6840±80	
Gd-6632	OES, Surface, 30 m SW of Grid A	6650±80	7000±80
Gd-5722	OES, Surface, 120 m S of Grid A	6120±70	6470±70
Gd-6645	CH, Grid B, NE of H-173, J11d	6640±80	
Gd-6638	CH, Grid B, H-173 Hearth under S wall, L12d	6920±80	
Gd-7088	OES, Surface, just W of Grid B	6990±70	7340±70

mud packing, the fact that hut entrances tend to be to the south, plus the care taken to shelter hearths from the north, suggest an abiding concern with the north wind, the prevailing, and often formidable, wind in the winter season.

The nature of the season of occupation, whether wet or dry, is more difficult to infer from the archaeological evidence. The location of the site, on the higher ground of an interfluve within a wadi system, together with the apparent avoidance by builders of the lowest area within the site, suggests a concern with flooding and points to a wet-season occupation. Further, the build-up of sandy (aeolian?) sediments between courses of rock, as found in several huts, suggests site abandonment during the dry season, assuming, of course, the abandonment was for only part of a year and not several years. On the other hand, the presence of laminated silts within structures (H-174 as well as H-2), might suggest wet- rather than dry-season abandonment. Regional palaeoclimatological evidence, for its part, does not resolve the issue. A study of charred wood from prehistoric sites across Egypt (Neumann 1989, and Figure 37) suggests that, between c. 7000 and 6500 bp, Dakhleh Oasis may have been virtually on the border between the area that had a winter wet season (storms from the Mediterranean) and that receiving summer rainfall (monsoons from the south). It is possible

of course that Dakhleh would have received precipitation from both sources.

Establishing the weather pattern of the season of occupation would help us determine the position of Locality 270 within the larger settlement pattern of its inhabitants. Several lines of evidence suggest that, the ambiguous faunal data notwithstanding, it was an oasis-floor aggregation site for pastoral groups who also used seasonal pastures atop the nearby plateau. Locality 270 is suggestively placed near a route to the top of the plateau, while the sheer size of the site, arguably housing several hundred people, suggests the population had moved beyond the pure hunter/gatherer stage to some form of food production (e.g. Smith 1992:34, 249). The nearby Locality 269, which appears to be an animal *kraal* (McDonald 1990b), suggests the keeping of herds or flocks. As for the 270 chipped stone collection, the distinctive scrapers, such as tranchets and side blow flakes, commonly found on later pastoralist sites in Dakhleh (McDonald 1990c), are present but rare on the site. If Locality 270 was in fact part of the annual round of a pastoral group, one might expect that plateau-top pastures would be exploited during and after a rainy season, and 270 and its environs, at the height of the dry season. Future work in and around Locality 270 will be geared to address some of these issues.

Holocene Prehistory: Interim Report
on the 1993 Season

Mary M. A. McDonald

In 1993, the field season for Holocene Prehistory ran for seven and a half weeks until 28 February. Aside from a some site survey in the general area, the focus as in the 1992 season was on Locality 270, a Bashendi Cultural Unit site with numerous stone circles found in south-eastern Dakhleh Oasis. Field time was divided between the mapping of structures in one portion of the site and excavation of a large pit-like feature that had been discovered in 1992. Faunal material from the site was analysed by C. S. Churcher and floral remains by U. Thanheiser. J. O'Carroll drew the artefacts, while A. J. Mills did the field photography and B. Churcher the object photography. My thanks to all of these, and to other DOP colleagues such as L. Krzyzaniak, K. Kroeper, C. A. Hope and M. Wiseman, who assisted with everything from chauffeuring services to fruitful discussions of the latest finds.

Map of the north-east portion of Locality 270

In 1992, a skeleton map of this sprawling site had been produced using a theodolite to plot in points for each of the structures and other features, as well as the outlines of nearby ridges and hills (McDonald and Walker, herein Figure 1). This year the job of 'fleshing out' these points was begun, with the plotting in of some of the structures themselves. The work focused on the north-eastern part of the site, where last year we had established a 20 by 24 m grid (Grid B). By running measuring tapes off the grid, and using the theodolite points as a check on accuracy, all the structures in that end of the site, within c. 80 m of the grid, were plotted in. The result (Figure 1) is a map of some 60 structures, 30% of the total, showing size, shape and orientation of each structure.

This mapped area is the lowest portion of the site, except for the basin just to the south-west, and an area

with, in addition to the features on the surface, up to one-half metre of *in situ* deposits, including buried structures (McDonald & Walker, herein). It is also the part of the site where the surface structures seem in greatest disrepair, with sections of walls apparently robbed out or otherwise damaged. Accordingly, a certain amount of interpretation has gone into the map, and questionable stretches of wall are outlined with dotted, rather than solid, lines.

Other mapped features, in addition to the structures, include small bin-like items, < 2 m to the side, one lying 20 m north of Grid B and another 35 m west of its south-west corner, apparent activity areas and other rock clusters of various sizes. One activity area, 7 by 3 m, at the north-east corner of Grid B, features, besides various stone slabs, burnt limestone cobbles, grinding slab fragments, a boulder mortar and several chipped-stone items including a pair of heavy-duty tools.

Within the mapped area, some clustering of structures is evident. To an extent this clustering may be governed by topography, but the groups show a coherence that probably reflects cultural input as well. The largest cluster is the grouping, 75 by 25 m, centred on Grid B. A second, circular or ring-shaped cluster, 25 m in diameter, lies to the west across the wadi. A third smaller grouping, just to the south of the latter, features units lying in a pattern rather like the cells in a honeycomb (Flannery 1972, 31).

Structures seem to differ somewhat from group to group. Those in the east cluster vary considerably in size and shape, and include several elongated ones up to 12 m in length. Those in the circular cluster are more uniform in size but include a pair of bilobed units. Structures in the cluster to the south of the latter are all quite small. Orientation is generally similar in all groups. Elongated ones tend to run east-west, while almost all have their openings to the south or south-east, no doubt reflecting the direction of the prevailing, northerly winds.

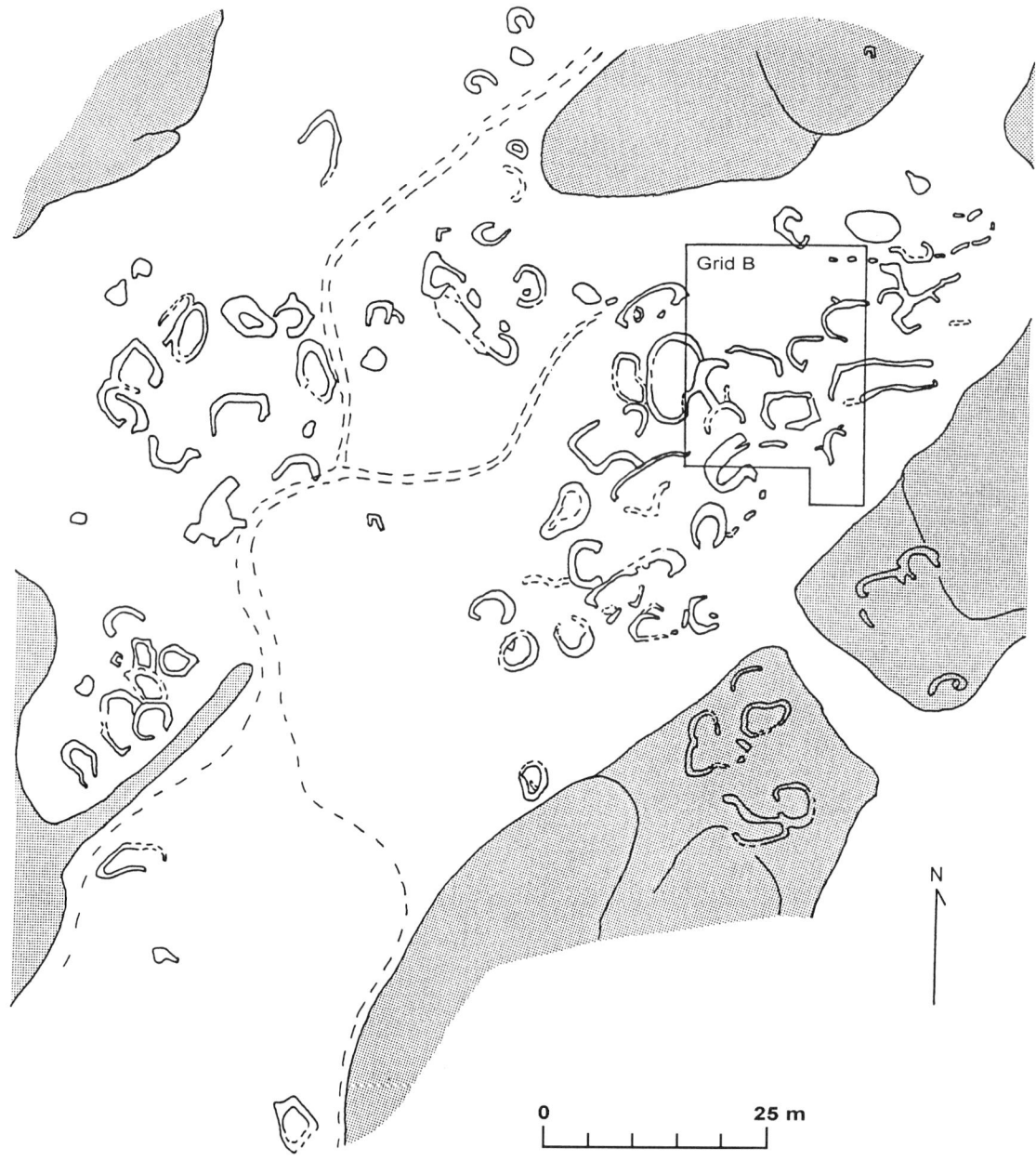

Figure 1 Locality 270: features in the north-east cluster.

Locality 270: Grid B Feature 1

Excavation of Feature 1

In addition to mapping structures and other surface phenomena, a goal in 1993 was the excavation of a large pit-like feature, Feature 1 (F-1), in the deposit of Grid B. Both the feature itself and the cultural debris it contained promised to shed further light on the history and function(s) of Locality 270. Aside from new artefacts to add to the collection from 1992, we needed economic data such as faunal material and especially plant remains. From the small faunal collection excavated in 1992, we had derived a species list, but no clear evidence either way concerning domestication. As for floral remains, with the exception of

one site in Nabta Playa, southern Egypt, dated 8000 bp (Wendorf et al. 1992), there is, because of the deflated state of most sites, virtually no information on plant use, other than charcoal from campfires (Neumann 1989) from anywhere in the Western Desert for the early to mid-Holocene.

Feature 1, which lies just west of Hut 173, had been cut into in 1992 while that structure was being excavated (McDonald and Walker, herein Figure 3; here, Figure 2a). The quantities of charcoal, ash and animal bone recovered from the slice of the pit lying within excavated squares J14 and K14 made F-1 a promising place to look for economic data. Accordingly, in 1993 the feature was

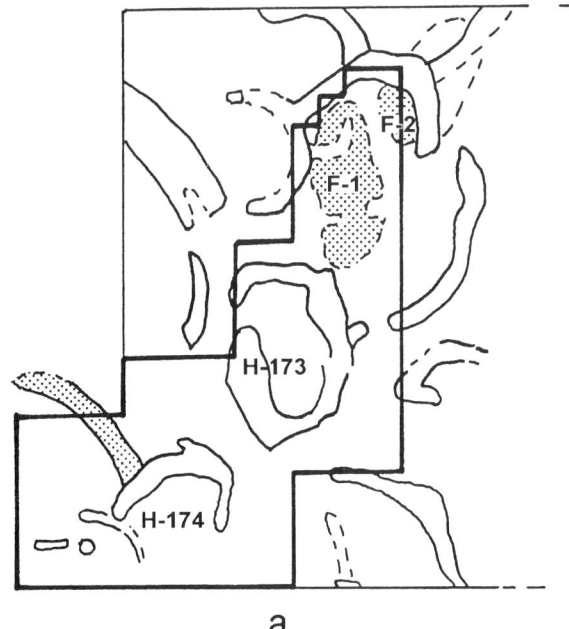

a

Figure 2 Locality 270: Grid B

a) Grid, south end: area worked 1992–93 (heavy line) and subsurface features (shaded).

b) F-1 and F-2: main grey layer and (darker shading) rocks and grey patch below it.

c) F-1 and F-2: mud-lump layer and overlying surface rocks.

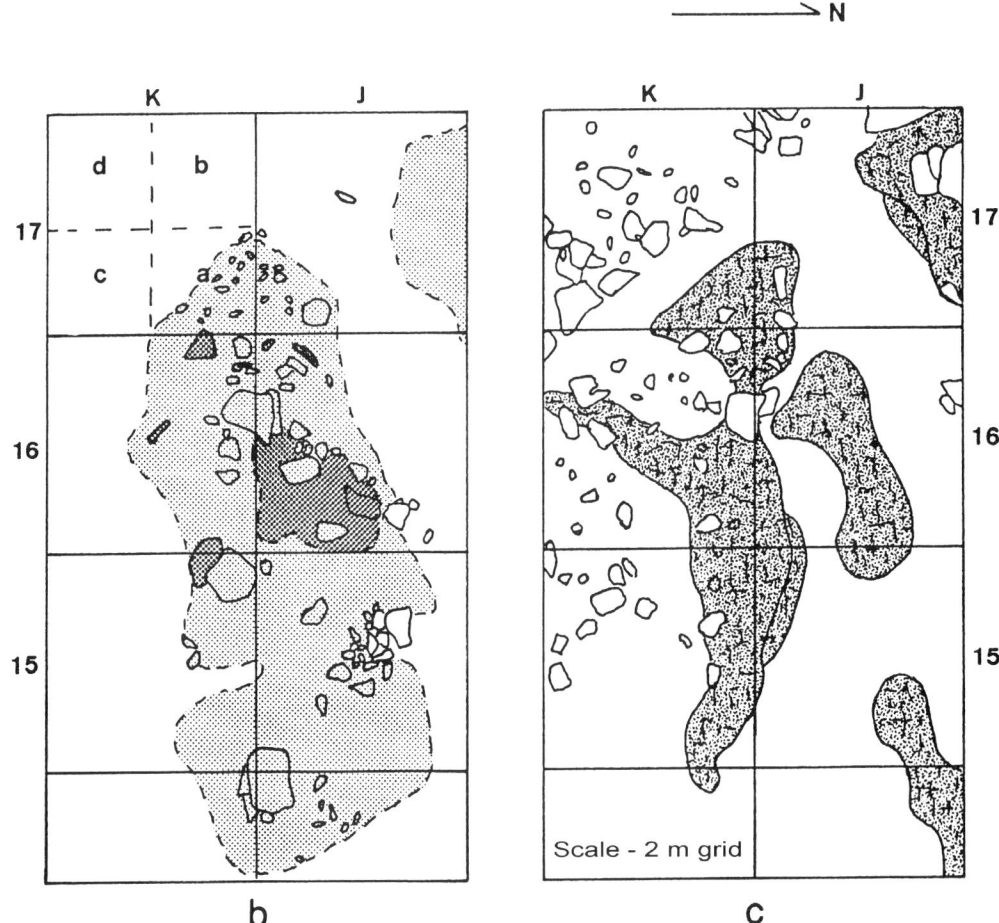

b

c

Figure 2 Locality 270: Grid B.

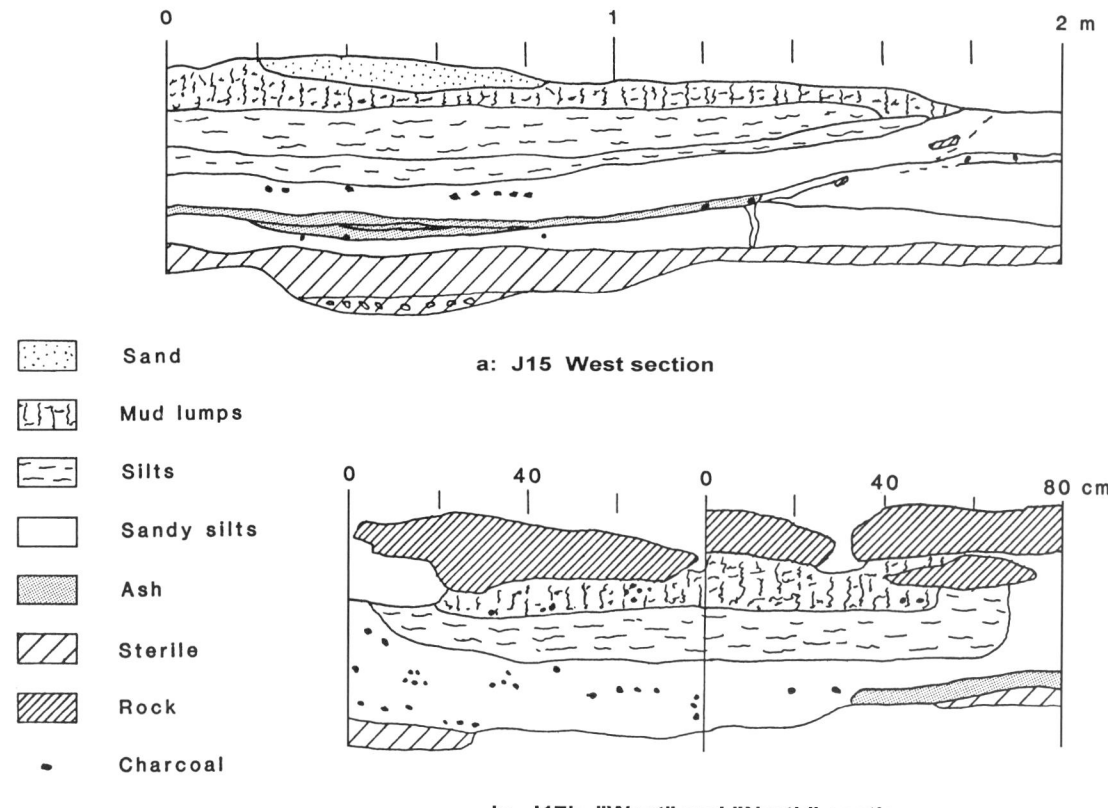

Figure 3 Locality 270: Grid B Sections a) Feature 1 and b) Feature 2.

excavated by peeling it down layer by layer, within each metre square. The excavated material was screened for artefacts and faunal remains, and a variety of deposits were sampled for floral material.

The feature proved to be a rough oval, c. 6 by 2 m, occupying or dug into a shallow basin. Four main layers could be detected within the 40 cm deep deposit: a thin grey layer near sterile soil which was overlain, first, by a deposit of reddish sandy silts with considerable charcoal, then by laminated silts, and, on the present surface, by a discontinuous layer of mud lumps (Figure 3a).

The lowest of these layers extends over most of the area covered by F-1 (Figure 2b). Two to four centimetres thick and slightly concave in cross section, it is a grey, ashy-looking deposit containing considerable charcoal. Reasonably intact over most of its area, it is thinner and somewhat fragmented, particularly towards its upturned edges. It is underlain in patches by lenses of red-stained sand. One of these patches, 80 by 40 cm, lies within square J15c; another is visible in the western section of J15. Smaller ones occur in J14. Sitting upon the grey layer are a number of stones of various sizes, some of them broken, others overlapping or stacked on lower ones. Some are red- or grey-stained. While most of the stones lie flat, a number of them, particularly towards the west end of F-1, are on edge, usually wedged deeply into the deposit under the grey layer.

One unusually dense cluster in the northern half of J15 proved to be a feature built well above the level of the grey layer. A section through the feature shows that several stones once stacked on the large stone in the north-western corner subsequently slid off, down slope, to the south-east. The north-west stone sits c.12 cm above the grey level, on a layer of silty muds, and there are muds as well between higher and lower stones within the tumble. The lowest rocks in the tumble, however, tilt down virtually to the grey layer, while that layer seems to be pinched out by the central part of the feature. There are many charcoal fragments in the muds under and around the tumbled rocks, and some of those rocks appear to be fire-stained.

The grey ashy layer does not sit directly on sterile soil. Between the two is a layer up to 12 cm thick, of variable hardness and sandiness, containing ash pockets, charcoal chunks and the occasional bone fragment. Within this deposit is at least one other grey ashy layer, similar to the higher one but much less extensive. In its present form this lower layer seems largely confined to square J16c (Figure 2b), but its presence as a second grey layer in sections under such rocks as the large one in the corner of K15b and that straddling the J14–J15 boundary, suggests it may once have covered a larger area. Rocks such as the southern of the two large ones in K15b are associated with this lower ashy layer, and the rocks on edge towards the western end of F-1 are wedged down at least to this level.

The 20–25 cm of deposit above the major, grey ashy layer and below the surface layer of mud lumps can for convenience sake be divided into two main layers, a sandier one below and one with laminated silts above. In fact each of these layers can be subdivided, with at least one surface appearing within each. Within each too are pockets of ash and of red-stained soil, patches where muds had collected, and a few rocks of various sizes, usually associated with a surface. Generally the silty deposits themselves tend to be free of artefacts and charcoal, but charcoal and the occasional bit of cultural debris can be found throughout the sandier layer.

Above the silts in F-1, on the present site surface, or in some cases under surface sands, is a layer of muds that break into desiccation polygons. These lumps, and the aeolian sand filling the cracks between them, contain no charcoal, stone or cultural debris. The mud layer, up to 12 cm thick, covers most but not all of the F-1 area (Figure 2c). The gaps between the patches of mud are filled with a soft, powdery deposit quite rich in charcoal, artefacts and small rocks. This latter deposit, like the mud lumps, sits upon the silt layer. Finally, this top layer of F-1, consisting of the combined mud-lump and powdery deposits, is capped in places by alignments of large rocks. This is most obvious in the western halves of squares K16 and J16, where a cluster of stones seems to form a small spur wall for the crescent-shaped Hut 191 to the west (Figures 2a–c). It appears that the distinctly-layered Feature 1 is not unique within Grid B. At the end of the 1993 season, the corner of a second pit (F-2) was cut into, about a metre from the first, in the northern half of square J17 (Figures 2a–c). This second feature seems roughly the same thickness as the first, and shows basically the same sequence of layers. A section within J17b (Figure 3b) shows a fragment of a grey ashy stratum, resting upon a layer of red-stained sand, overlain first by sandy silts, then laminated silts, and finally by a mud-lump layer, in this case with charcoal and some chipped stone amongst the lumps. This sequence in turn is capped by the large rocks of the arc-shaped H-191, which is aligned quite differently from the layered feature beneath it.

It is possible that a third such feature lies just to the north-east of F-1. In the western section of J14 (not illustrated), the northern edge of F-1 seems to be cut into by a layered pit, the bulk of which would lie to the north of J14. It is possible that the patch of muds on the surface in the north-western corner of J14 (Figure 2c) pertains to this postulated feature.

Finally, the deposit beyond the layered features described above seems fairly uniform throughout the area dug in 1993. Between 5–10 cm below the present surface of the site with its litter of artefacts is a second surface sparsely scattered with chipped stone and rocks, most of them small. To the south-east of F-1, in the eastern half of K15, are two post moulds, 10 and 12 cm in diameter, and 80 cm apart, that may originate at this level. It appears this might be an early surface associated with the structures on the Grid B surface. Below it is 'Level 1', a fairly loose deposit c. 8–10 cm thick, with some charcoal and grey patches, which is underlain in turn by harder, more granular reddish soil (Level 2). In K15, with the largest exposure of this material, the top of the reddish deposit shows several features probably originating in the overlying greyer layer; a pit 50 cm across containing a couple of small rocks on edge and a few lithics, a similar, slightly smaller pit, another soft area measuring 40 by 75+ cm, and a red-stained patch 20 cm in diameter. Finally, it is somewhat difficult to establish the exact stratigraphic relationship between F-1 and the deposit lying beyond it, given the limited exposure of the latter, and the fact that the crucial layers are all very close to the present surface. The one section that may shed light on the matter, the western section of J15 (Figure 3a), seems to show the extension of the major grey layer of F-1 lying between what would be the soft greyish deposit of Level 1 and the harder reddish material beneath it.

Economic Data

Information on activities in and around Feature 1 comes from floral and faunal remains, chipped- and ground-stone items, and a few artefacts in other material such as ostrich eggshell, bone and clay. In 1993, 21 soil samples were collected for archaeo-botanical analysis. Nineteen of these, plus one from the 1992 season, are from F-1, where all the layers have been sampled, and the other two are from F-2. While no detailed results are available yet, preliminary reports indicate that plant macrofossils (grass seeds) have been preserved. The faunal list from the 1993 season includes a mollusc, small rodents, assumed to be intrusive, small and medium size birds, and possibly a small carnivore. Also present are dorcas gazelle, goat or sheep,[1] and a larger animal, the size of a hartebeest or small cow. The mollusc, *Pila ovata*, is a freshwater animal and suggests the presence of water and grass. As for distribution, all species except for the mollusc occur in F-1, while all except the large mammal, but including the mollusc, were found in the small section of F-2 excavated to date.

A total of 990 pieces of chipped stone were recovered in 1993. Of these, 56 are formal tools, another 11 heavy duty items, while 63 could be classed as informal or use-retouched items. There are also 12 cores, four of them bipolar, 16 core fragments, and two hammerstone fragments. Cores and core fragments are both more common than in the larger collection from 1992 (McDonald & Walker, herein) and suggest that flint knapping was one

---

[1] This material was re-examined in 1998 and proved to be gazelle. To date then, no caprines have been identified at Locality 270 (Churcher, C. S., 1998, personal communication).

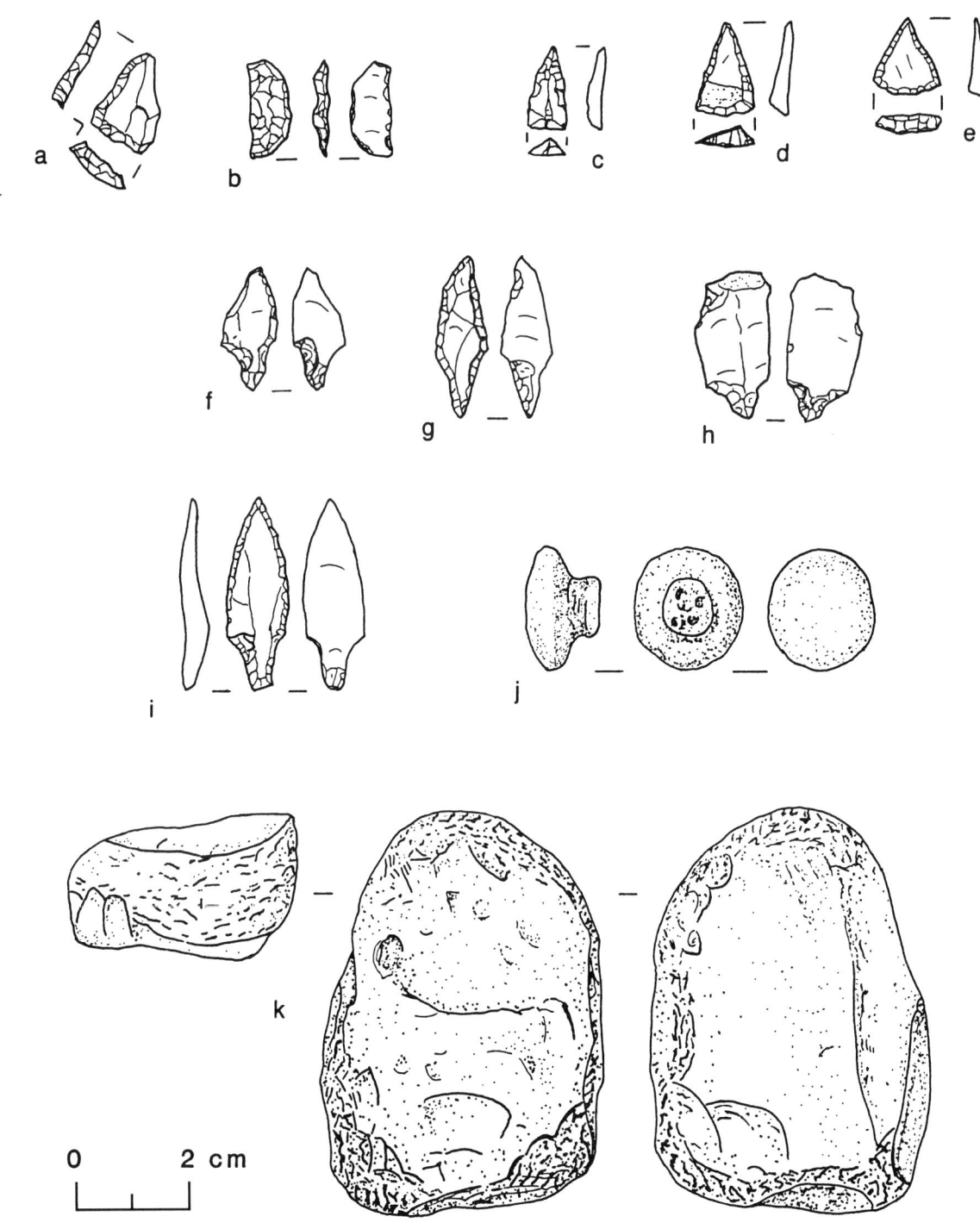

0 2 cm

Figure 4 Locality 270: Grid B artefacts in and around Feature 1.

Table 1 Percentage frequencies of chipped-stone-tool classes in collections from Locality 270: entire 1992 and 1993 collections, and a portion of the 1993 collection from Feature 1.

	1992	1993	F-1
Arrowheads	16.9	28.6	36.8
Notches	5.6	12.5	5.3
Denticulates	7.0	10.7	7.9
Piercers	25.3	14.3	15.8
Drills	1.4	1.7	2.6
Combinations	2.8	16.1	15.8
Scrapers	1.4	–	–
Knives	5.6	–	–
W/retouch	23.9	10.7	7.9
Burins	4.2	1.7	2.6
Geometrics	4.2	3.6	5.3
Planes	1.4	–	–
Number	71	56	38

of the activities carried out in F-1. Table 1 lists the tool classes found so far on Locality 270 and the percentage frequencies from several worked areas. The most prominent categories in and around F-1, aside from the arrowheads, are piercers, notches and denticulates; the combination tools consist mostly of these three elements as well. The 'geometrics' category consists of triangles and lunates (Figure 4a, b). Two types of arrowhead are present, triangular-shaped and tanged, both small. The triangles, all under 2 cm, are isosceles-shaped, with mostly unifacial, direct-edge retouch on all three edges (Figure 4c–e). The tanged items, all but one under 3 cm long, are fairly simple, with bifacial-edge retouch mostly confined to the tang (Figure 4f–i). One or two appear unfinished. The arrowheads recovered from the nearby Huts 173 and 174 in 1992 are similar to the 1993 collection in all major respects.

The heavy-duty tools, up to 10 cm long, tend to be made on thick-sectioned, parallel-sided nodules of quartzite, cherty limestone or ferruginous sandstone (Figure 4k). The edges, in several cases roughly sharpened by flaking, show subsequent heavy damage from battering or rubbing. Six of these tools were found within the F-1 deposits, two of them sitting on the main grey layer.

As with the areas around the structures dug in 1992, the F-1 location featured no complete grinding slabs or handstones; unlike the former areas, however, it did yield nine grindstone fragments, two of them broken handstones, the rest slab fragments. The two largest, 17 and 21 cm across, probably from the same slab although they do not conjoin, were found about two metres apart, sitting on the major F-1 grey layer. On each fragment, both sides are ground smooth, and all ground surfaces show zones or patches of pecking damage. The other slab fragments, all much smaller, also show pecking damage on smoothed grinding surfaces.

Other categories of artefact found in 1993 include ostrich-eggshell beads, a pair of bone tools, an item in calcite, and a few fragments of impressed clay. A total of 76 ostrich-eggshell beads and bead fragments were recovered around F-1. While 68% are surface finds, they come also from virtually all layers in F-1, from F-2, and from *in situ* deposits beyond both. They may not have been manufactured on this spot, however: ostrich-eggshell fragments are relatively rare around F-1, only one bead seemed unfinished; and the excavation yielded a single stone drill, a tool generally more common on spots where beads were being made.

Two slim bone awls were found in 1993, one in each of the two features. The F-2 awl is 4.3 cm long and 0.35 cm in diameter at its wide end. From the edge of F-2 came a button or stud of calcite, its head 2.1 by 1.9 cm, and measuring 1.35 cm from front to back (Figure 4j). Finally, while no sherds as such were found in 1993, several small fragments of impressed mud, none measuring over 2.5 cm, were recovered from both F-1 and F-2 deposits. Some of these bear what appear to be reed or mat impressions, while one shows the finer imprint of what may be basketry or even impressed pottery.

Discussion

Concerning the function of layered phenomena such as Feature 1, two main possibilities come to mind. One is that these are former structures, like the stone rings found on the surface of Locality 270 today. As with another still-intact buried structure just to the east in Grid B, running under H-174 (Figure 2a; McDonald & Walker, herein), they would have been lived in for a while, perhaps repeatedly. But when F-1 was finally abandoned, most of the wall stones would be removed for another structure, leaving the discontinuous pattern of stone seen in Figure 2b.

One problem with this suggestion is that there is really little reflection of a perimeter wall in the pattern of stones associated with the main grey surface. Rather, most of the rocks are found towards the centre of the feature, and a number of large, presumably useful ones, remain in place. The extensive burning represented particularly by the major grey layer also seems inconsistent with the idea of a covered dwelling, unless it reflects a conflagration that destroyed the structure, an event for which there is otherwise little evidence. Another possibility is that Feature 1 represents a special activity area involving considerable burning and the use of a heavy-duty tool kit. In the case of the major grey layer, the fires seem coextensive with the feature itself, but burnt patches above and below this layer, and apparently otherwise similar to it, seem much less extensive. Many of the rocks sitting on or below the grey layer, then, might have served to shelter fires. The row of stones running diagonally across J16 coincide with the north-western boundary of the lowest grey patch and they may have continued in use as a shelter for the successor fires of the major layer. Likewise, the tumble of rocks in J15 might be interpreted as a small wind shelter (it is only about 45 cm wide south-west to north-east) consisting of a pile of rocks sitting upon a mud platform. One of the major patches of red-stained sand lies just downwind of this feature. The stones may have tumbled in a period of site abandonment, trapping silts from a puddle filling the hollow where the hearth had been.

The purpose of these postulated fires remains unclear. This does not appear to be a major meat-processing area; there are at best a few small scraps of bone around, and there is little evidence of knives or scrapers. The analysis of plant remains from these ashy, charcoal-filled deposits may provide further information on the matter. As for tools, the presence of cores, core fragments and hammerstones in the ashy layers suggests that ordinary chippedstone tools were required here. The most prominent feature of the lithic assemblage, though, is the heavy-duty tool kit. The several grindstone fragments with pecking marks, and cobbles with battering or rubbing damage on their edges, suggest some special type of processing within F-1. Just as it is unclear what activities produced the deposit and assemblages in the lower levels, the upper layers of

F-1 remain somewhat mysterious. The laminated silts may be a natural deposit representing periods of site abandonment. As for the mud-lump layer, whether or not it too is a natural deposit, and its relationship to the lower layers of F-1, remain to be determined.

There is evidence from adjacent squares, as mentioned above, that the layered F-1 is not unique. In addition, there are signs of what appear to be similar burning episodes elsewhere in Grid B. Two of these underlie the nearby H-173 and one of them yielded virtually the only grindstone fragments recovered on 270 during the 1992 season (McDonald and Walker, herein). What may be a similar burnt feature was found on another part of 270, under Hut 4 in Grid A.

Finally, as mentioned above, F-1 and F-2 have both been built over by structures on the present surface of Locality 270, structures aligned quite differently than the layered features below them. This same pattern of stone-built structures overlying the distinctive burnt features, not all of them however with the overlying strata of F-1, seems to occur elsewhere on Grid B, and on at least one other spot within this sprawling site. This evidence suggests that Locality 270 might have undergone a change in function within its life history, from being primarily an industrial site to a largely residential one.

'Ein Birbiyeh

Anthony J. Mills

At the Roman period temple known as 'Ein Birbiyeh, site 31/435–K5–1 (for which see, most recently, Mills 1990a), the work undertaken was principally in the area between the hypostyle area and the gateway (Figure 1). Work at this site was begun in 1982, when it was first inspected during the survey (Mills 1983, 132–4). At that time it was realised that the gateway was decorated with relief carvings and that the façade of the main temple building had a frieze of uraei along the exterior surface of its screen wall. There was also a fragment of an inscription which led us to believe that the screen wall was also decorated with relief. In the 1990–1991 season, the upper 0.50 m was excavated from inside the area marked A-B-C (Mills 1990a, 16) and a frieze of carved uraei was discovered at the top of the inner face of the screen wall. This led us to believe that the screen wall had carved relief decoration on the inside as well as the exterior.

The first work to be undertaken on site, in 1992, was the completion of the epigraphic recording of the gateway inscriptions and scenes by Olaf E. Kaper. Following this, the gateway was refilled with clean sand. This is a protective measure which will serve to support the gateway structure and surfaces, and at the same time, prevent damage by environmental or human agency. Of course, it can be removed at any time without damaging or endangering the gateway structure.

Adam Zielinski and Anthony J. Mills concentrated efforts on the investigation of the area between the inner side of the gateway piers and the outer face of the screen wall, partly to discover what lay between the two elements of the temple and partly to determine the decoration of the screen wall.

The surface of this area was packed mud, with an irregular contour that was levelled by blown-in sand. The tops of the screen wall and its columns were just discernible on the same surface as the top of the gateway. The area was bounded by a short east-west wall at the northern side, adjacent to the North Outer Corridor, with no enclosing wall discernible at the southern edge; the western side was the façade of the temple and the eastern was the gateway and the mud-brick wall mass that lies adjacent to it.

A trench was excavated up to 2.90 metres in depth.

There was considerable uniformity of fill throughout this section, with various features in it. The fill consisted of very hard (?mineralized) clay which bore quantities of sherd material and little else, interleaved with a crumbly burnt clay debris. Colours of this burning range from black through grey to brick-orange. These burning features ascend to the surface in places and elsewhere are as deep as the trench bottom. Throughout, this deposit, which obviously represents some industrial activity, sits without flooring or discernible lenses of occupation or activity debris. It is almost as if all the fill had been dumped into a huge pit, sometimes with burning or burnt clay, sometimes not.

The screen wall, a feature of major interest, is nowhere decorated. At the top of the wall is a series of uraei, 0.50 m high, which sit on a squared plinth held up by a cornice. Twenty-five centimetres below the cornice is a torus moulding surrounding a space which would normally have been decorated. This space was finished to a smoothed surface. The screen wall, with uraei at the top, is continued across the end of the South Outer Corridor, forming a continuous façade from the entrance doorway to the 'Porch' across to the exterior wall of the Southern Corridor. There was no apparent access into the Southern Corridor through this extension of the screen wall.

At a depth of 1.25 m a stone wall was found closing the space at the southern end. It is very slightly out of alignment with the south wall of the Southern Outer Corridor, which may be the result of ground movement. Within the 1.22 m thickness of this wall an entrance 1.26 m wide gives into a rectangular niche, 1.50 m by 0.57 m. Although the eastern end of this wall was unexcavated, the niche appears to have been in the centre of the wall. The interior faces of the niche are all smooth-dressed. Presumably, it was a space for a large, standing cult icon or some similar object.

The top of the screen wall was traced throughout the northern half of the 'Porch' and is similarly configured to that on the south half, with uraei between each pillar or wall. This is expected, as it concludes the normal symmetry of Egyptian temple architecture.

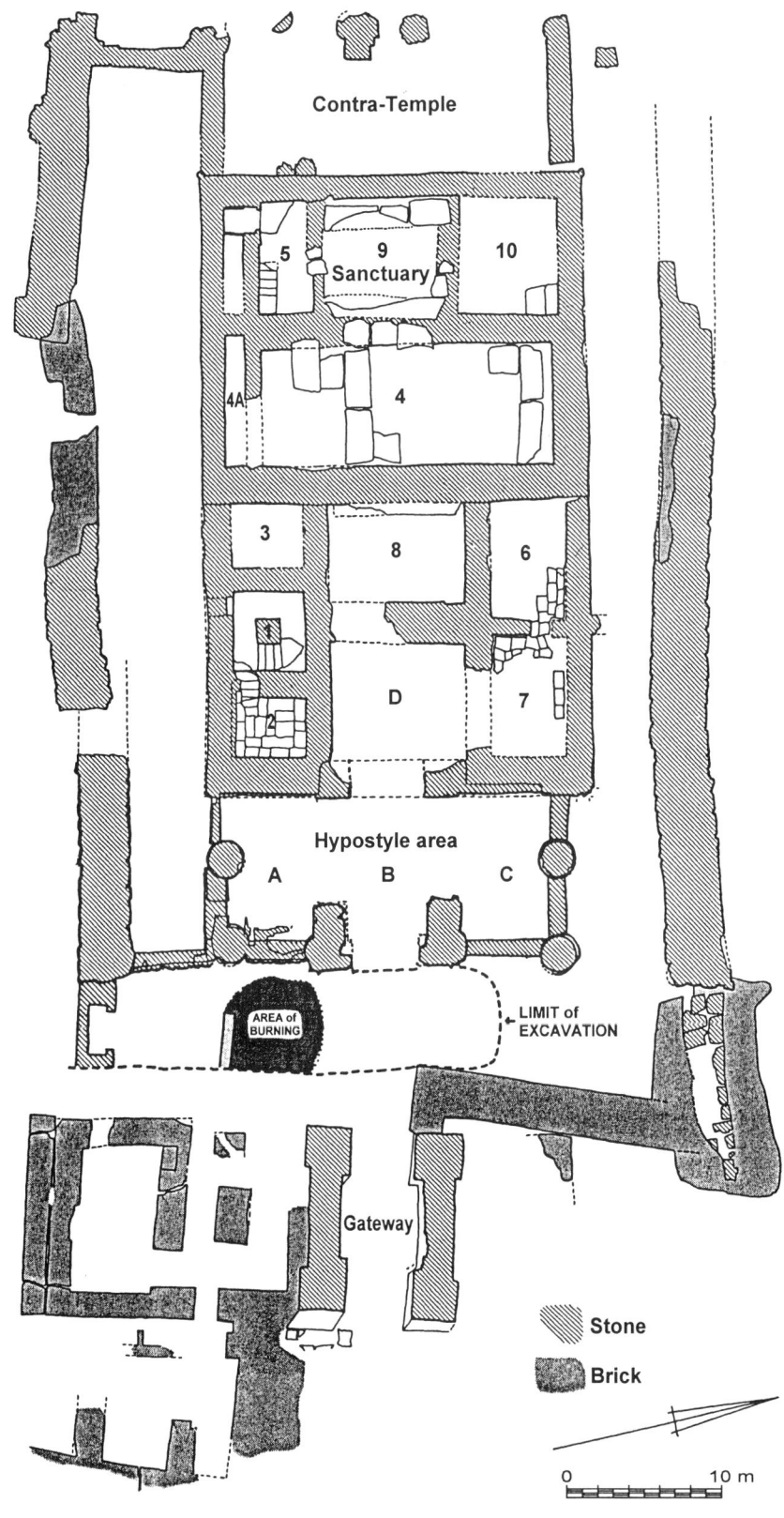

Figure 1 The Temple of ʿEin Birbiyeh, 31/435-K5-1.

Deir el-Haggar

Anthony J. Mills

The rehabilitation of the temple at Deir el-Haggar, begun last season as a joint activity of the Dakhleh Oasis Project together with the Egyptian Antiquities Organization (Mills 1990b, 20–3), was continued through the two seasons presented here. During this period, the Hypostyle Hall and the western three rooms of the temple were cleared to floor level. The debris everywhere was a combination of blown sand with some fallen building materials, which latter were mainly on, or close to, the surface. Remelé, the photographer with the Rohlfs Expedition in 1874–5, excavated the Sanctuary chamber and removed the decorated ceiling blocks.[1] As a result of this activity, the Sanctuary chamber was relatively free of sand and there was no other debris in the room.

Although this work has not been treated as an archaeological study, a number of the results have been very interesting. Penetrating the temenos wall there are eight doorways, as well as the stone-built, Main Gateway in the centre of the mud-brick pylon. Each of the doorways is about 1.20 m wide and they are regularly spaced, three in each of the northern and southern walls and one on either side of the Main Gateway. The purpose of these doorways cannot generally be ascertained, although the one that penetrates the temenos south of the Main Gateway, where a series of large graffiti can be seen, might have been a popular or festival entrance. The graffiti include several depictions of rams and baboons, an ibis and two depictions of Heron, a warrior deity. There are also several Greek texts in this doorway.

The inner surface of the temenos wall and the Processional Way colonnade was plastered and painted in a variety of colours, generally each column had two colours and no two adjacent columns were painted the same.

Within the temple building, only the doorways, and some of the walls, facing the processional axis were decorated with relief carving. More interesting, perhaps, is the fact that the temple continued throughout its use as a ritual building in an unfinished condition. The eastern, northern and southern walls of the Porch of Titus, of the Hypostyle Hall, and of the Hall of Offerings are all unfinished, the stone being left roughly dressed with the mortar that had run out of the joints left uncleaned from the faces of the stones. Only one of the four columns in the Hypostyle Hall (the north-eastern one) has been smoothed. Of additional interest is the great amount of black, hard but fragile deposit which has been left on all parts of the processional axis. The columns and doorjambs (finished and unfinished) of this central axis all bear deposits of this substance and the thresholds of the doorways also have considerable quantities of it. The floor of the Sanctuary had a particularly thick deposit all around the barque stand.

The southern wall of the Main Temple was intact to the cornice, as was the western wall. The northern wall of the Hypostyle Hall and the Hall of Offerings had, however, collapsed outwards. Fortunately, it all fell altogether. By carefully mapping the position of each fallen block and numbering each before removal to a storage area, the juxtaposition of many of the wall blocks was preserved. An additional help was the fact that each course was a different height from its neighbours, and courses could be sorted out by these measurements. Finally, the first-century masons had marked on each lower course by scratching a line, the position of the blocks above. It was with confidence that we were able to reconstruct this undecorated wall as high as the window level.

As the ancient masons had used a lime mortar for their block joints, so we used this material, rather than an ugly, hard cement. The lime was mixed with clean sand for this purpose and will be as good as the original. In addition, all of the joints between blocks were cleaned out and repointed with lime mortar.

It is our intention to complete work at Deir el-Haggar next season and to return the site to the Egyptian Government authorities. We will leave the site cleared of debris, safe for the visitors, and the monument protected from both natural and human agencies as much as possible. There will also be a Visitor Information Centre which will explain the site in simple terms so that the visitor will have a more instructed, and thereby a more interesting, site visit.

---

[1] Winlock (1936, 6) mentions a graffito by Remelé recording this activity.

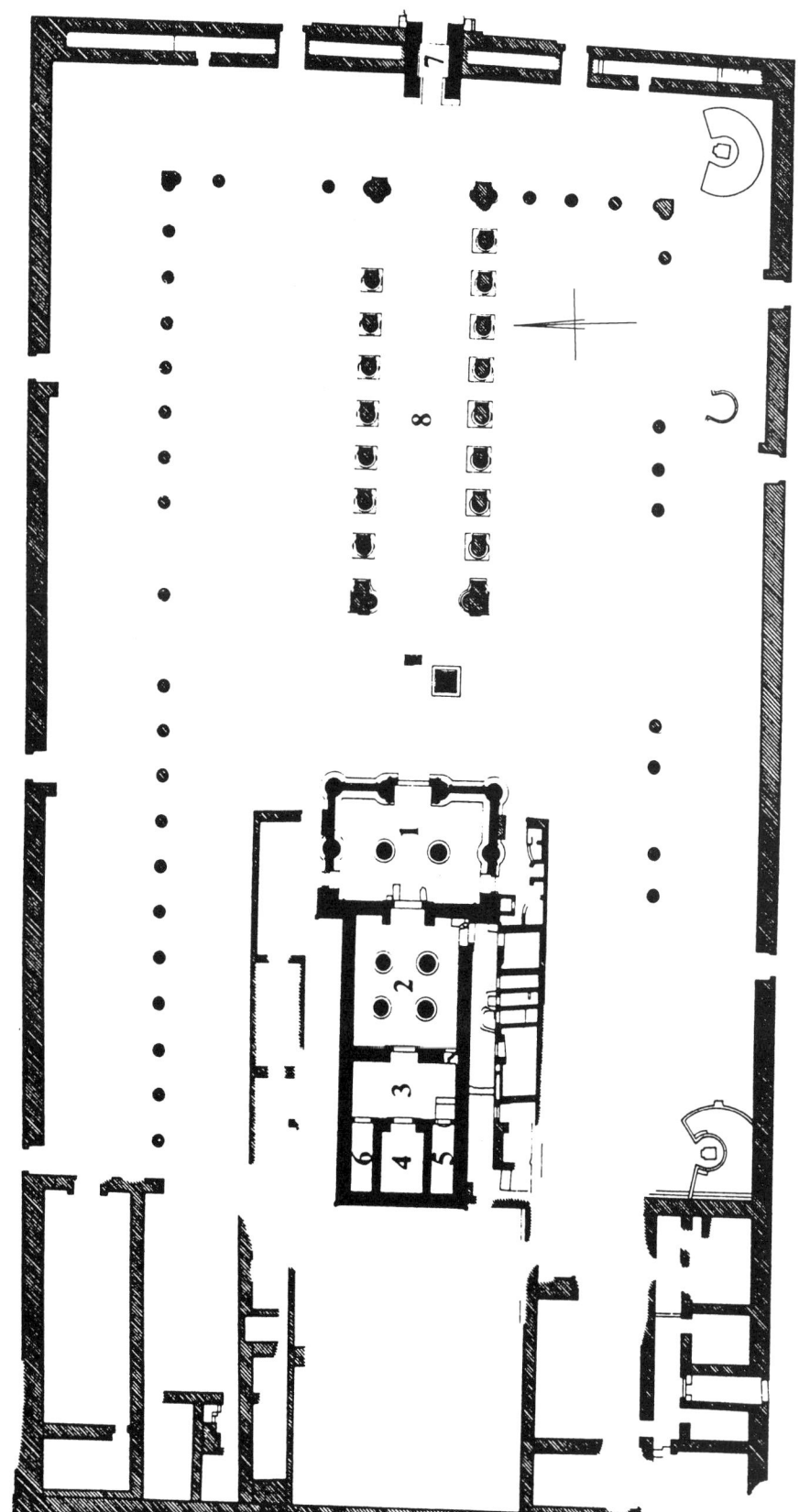

Plan of the Temple at Deir el-Haggar.

(J. E. Knudstad)

The Excavations at Ismant el-Kharab (ancient Kellis): Settlement and Cemeteries

Excavations in the Cemeteries
of Ismant el-Kharab

Michael Birrell

Two cemeteries associated with the settlement of Ismant el-Kharab have been partially excavated by the Dakhleh Oasis Project during four field seasons: 11–14 February 1991, 18–29 February 1992, 17 November to 12 December 1992 and 24 November to 15 December 1993. Archaeologists on site were P. Sheldrick, Chatham, Ontario, E. C. Brock, Canadian Institute in Cairo, and M. Birrell, Macquarie University. The physical anthropologists were J. E. Molto, Lakehead University, and S. Fairgrieve, Laurentian University. Preliminary soft tissue analysis was undertaken by M. Cook, Henry Ford Hospital, C. A. Marlow, University of Durham, and M. Zimmerman, University of Pennsylvania. Full autopsies of mummified remains were made by A. Aufderheide and M. Zlonis, University of Minnesota, and L. Cartmell of Ada, Oklahoma. Ceramics were studied by C. A. Hope, Monash University/Museum of Victoria, and S. F. Patten, Macquarie University. The palaeobotanist was U. Thanheiser, University of Vienna. Work on site was facilitated by representatives of the Egyptian Antiquities Organization, notably Ashraf es-Sayed Mohammed.

The two cemeteries are located north of the settlement, on either side of the *wadi* which runs from the north-east to the west of the settlement (Hope 1988, 162). The cemetery west of the wadi (referred to herein as the West Cemetery), consists of a large number of small chamber tombs. It is designated 31/420–C5–1[1] by the Dakhleh Oasis Project and is assigned to the Ptolemaic and early Roman periods on the basis of its ceramic and other artefactual material. The East Cemetery (31/420–C5–2), located on a broad plain east of the wadi, consists of simple rectangular pit graves cut into the red Nubian clay, some of which retain mud-brick superstructures and enclosure walls (Mills 1982, 99). The graves in the area of the cemetery excavated

so far are tentatively dated to the late third to early fourth centuries CE.

The West Cemetery (31/420–C5–1)

The West Cemetery is located in a progression of low hills to the north-west of Ismant el-Kharab. The hills form the western edge of a *wadi* which runs from the north-east to the south-west of the settlement. The predominant geological matrix of the area is the red Nubian clay. This is capped in the higher sections of the hills by a 50–60 cm stratum of friable green-grey shales, overlaid by another of orange-white, fine-grained sandstone.[2] The area is covered with a fine layer of sand and randomly scattered flint nodules. Bleached bones and pottery sherds from disturbed graves are also present on the surface. The hills are relatively steep, rising 6–8 m above the *wadi* bed, to a height of 126 m above sea level.

The excavations in the West Cemetery have been concentrated in a 200 m section of the hills between the Mut–Balat road, which passes through them, and the mouth of a subsidiary wadi. The cemetery is far more extensive, spreading to the south-west and north, with its limits yet to be defined. The area under investigation is a weathered north-south terrace of sandstone and shale rising 6 m above the level of the *wadi* bottom. Three small hills of red Nubian clay on the eastern side of the terrace and a clay outcrop immediately north of the Mut–Balat road have also been excavated.

Preliminary investigations took place in under the supervision of P. Sheldrick during February 1991. More detailed investigation took place in the following two seasons when, together with E. C. Brock, he excavated

---

[1] Originally numbered 31/420-C6-1; for a brief description see Mills 1982, 98.

[2] The strata are similar to those described by Zittel in his observations of the geology around Tenida, given in Beadnell 1901, 79.

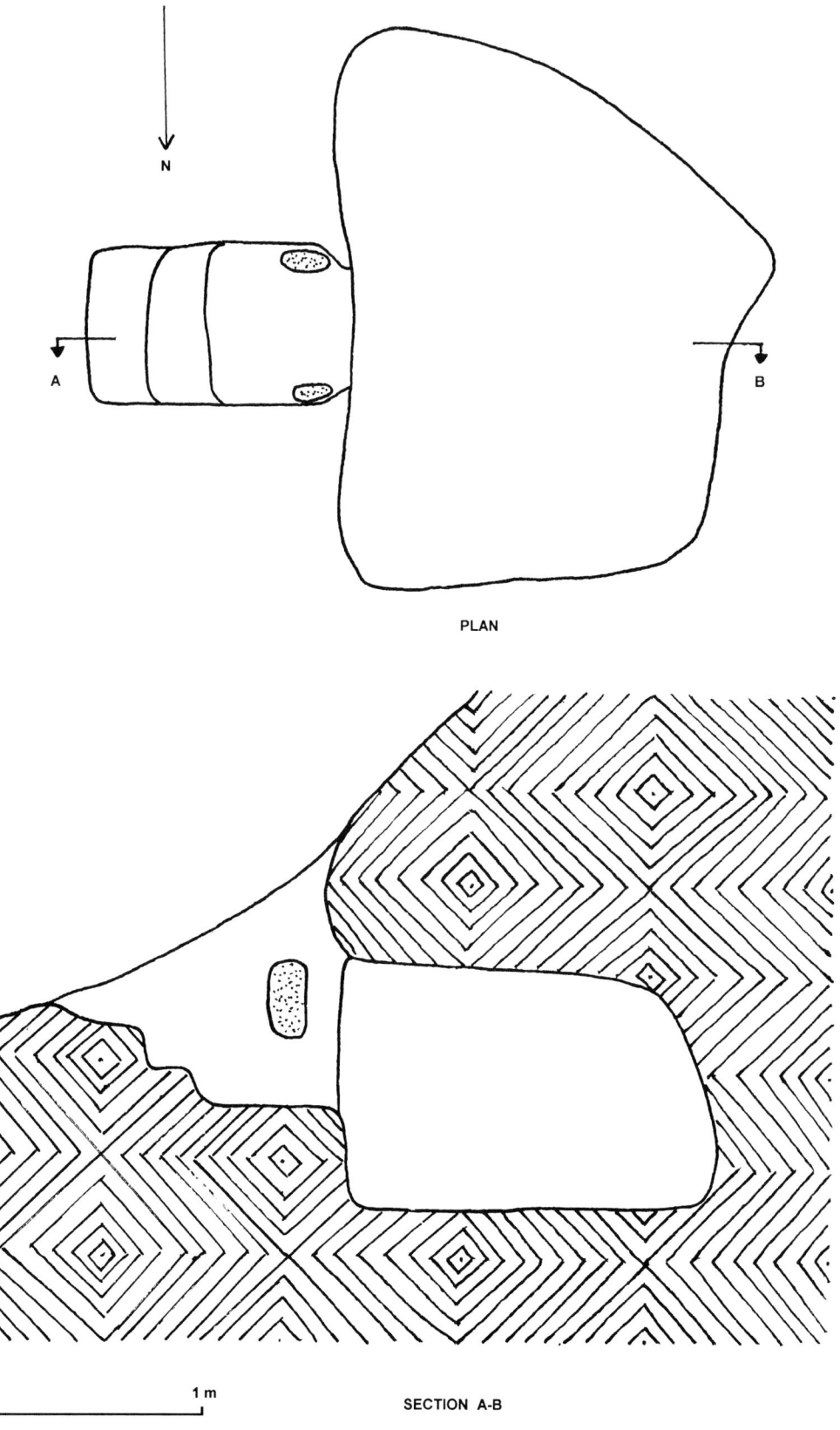

Figure 1 West Cemetery: Tomb 9 plan and section.

Tombs 1–6. In March 1993, E. C. Brock cleared Tomb 7, a structure which had been recently damaged by earth-moving equipment during road works, and later that year M. Birrell and P. Sheldrick excavated a further eight chamber tombs (Tombs 8–15).

The 15 tombs can be divided into two basic groups depending on their physical location in the cemetery: Group 1 tombs are cut entirely into the red Nubian clay and Group 2 tombs are those dug into the clay of the higher sandstone terrace.

Group 1

Eight of the tombs which have been excavated were cut entirely into the red clay hills east of the sandstone terrace, and in the isolated outcrop north of the road: Tombs 1–4, 5, 7, 9, and 12. The tombs in this group are situated in close proximity, taking advantage of all available space. They have no particular orientation but follow the contours of the hills.

The entrance to each tomb consists of a deep, narrow passage carved from the Nubian clay. An example is Tomb 9 which has an entry passage 130 cm long and 70 cm wide, descending in three steps of uneven height to 50 cm below the surface (Figure 1). In Tomb 1 the steps are reinforced with mud bricks. The sides of the entrance passage are coated with a smearing of mud plaster or are lined with mud bricks. In some tombs (e.g. Tomb 5), a mud-brick arch was apparently built over the entrance.

Roughly-carved sandstone blocks are occasionally inserted into the walls of the entrance passage on either side of the doorway, often at a considerable height above the floor of the passage (Figure 1). This is the situation in Tombs 1, 3 and 12. The stones are held in place by a coarse mud plaster. A roughly-squared sandstone block was used to seal each tomb, usually placed up against the door jambs (Plate 1). The jambs of Tomb 1 have narrow grooves cut into their outer surfaces, indicating that a portcullis stone was placed between them, though no such stone was found *in situ*. Tomb 1 also had a wooden door at some stage, since a door socket was found plastered between sandstone slabs just within the entrance.

A step of 45 cm or less gives access from the entrance passage to the floor of each chamber. The dimensions of Tomb 2 are fairly typical and will serve as an example: 365 cm long by 260 cm wide, with a maximum ceiling height of 100 cm. The walls and ceilings of the tombs are slightly curved to give stability. A few tombs have pillars of native clay retained to ensure the strength of the ceiling (e.g. Tomb 5) or have separate chambers divided by walls (Tomb 1). Natural faults in the clay structure of the walls were filled with mud bricks plastered over with mud.

Tomb 5 has two shallow pits in the southern extension of the chamber. The pits have a north-south axis and are quite shallow; the western one is 92 cm by 54 cm with a depth of 22 cm. They were designed presumably for burials of children.

The shape of these tombs is similar to those excavated at ʿEin Tirghi, and now dated to the Ptolemaic Period on

Plate 1 West Cemetery: Tomb 12 entrance.

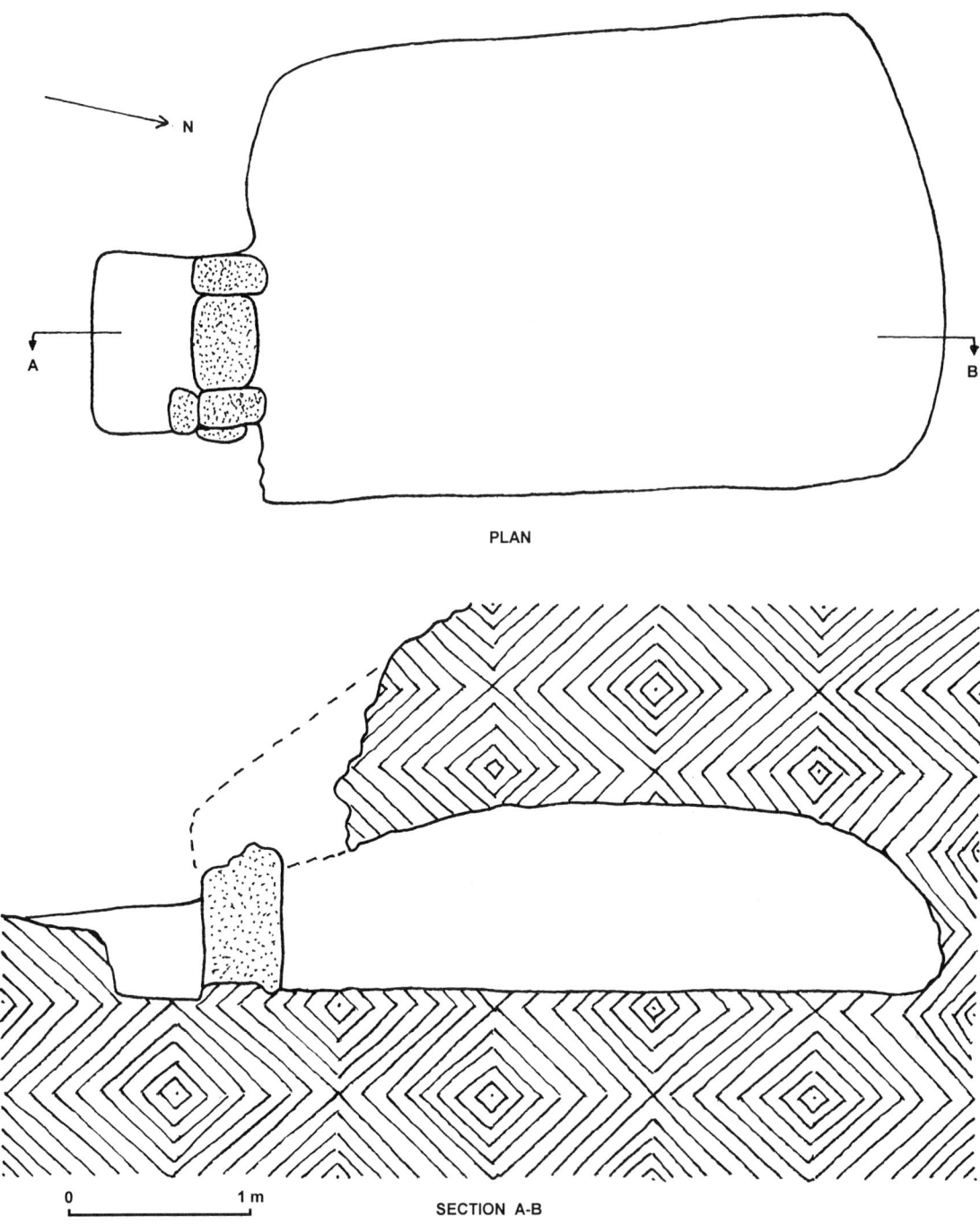

PLAN

SECTION A-B

Figure 2 West Cemetery: Tomb 8 plan and section.

the basis of the ceramic material (Tombs 33, 35 and 37; see Frey 1986, 93, fig. 2). The continuity of this architectural form is clearly a result of the material in which they are carved.

Group 2

The sandstone terrace to the west contains less regularly-spaced tombs, carved into the red clay beneath the shale and sandstone strata. Such tombs are: Tomb 6, 8, 10, 11,

14 and 15. Tomb 13 is carved into the clay hill south of the entrance of the subsidiary wadi but the form of the entrance passage, the artefacts in the tomb and the treatment of the bodies link it with the tombs of this group.

The tombs have no regular orientation but follow the contour of the shale stratum. The entrance passage is carved into the red clay and consists of a circular or roughly squared pit up to 80 cm in diameter and normally only about 30 cm deep (Tomb 8). The doorway is furnished with roughly-squared sandstone jambs, a

Plate 2 West Cemetery: Tomb 8 entrance.

sandstone threshold embedded into the clay and a lintel supported by the jambs. All of the stonework was held in place by mud plaster (Plate 2). The entrance to each tomb was blocked with a sandstone slab placed against the outer face of the doorjambs or a block inserted into a groove in the doorjambs (Tomb 15). In all examples the blocking stone was either pushed back from its intended position or was missing altogether.

The chambers are small, very roughly-carved rectangular rooms with low ceilings. There is normally no step from the level of the entrance passage to the surface of the tomb floor. The dimensions of Tomb 8 are typical of its group: 370 cm long by 220 cm wide and a maximum ceiling height of 98 cm (Figure 2). In many cases the shale and sandstone strata of the façade was reinforced with sandstone and mud-brick walls near the entrance (Tombs 8 and 11). Natural faults in the walls were filled with mud bricks and small stones plastered over with mud (Tomb 11). The sandstone above the door of each tomb had been subjected to erosion, enabling wind-blown sand to accumulate inside, normally to within 15–20 cm of the roof.

Tomb 15 is unusual amongst those in Group 2 in having a recess carved into one wall. This is located at floor level in the south wall and is 30–50 cm wide, 190 cm long and 43 cm high. From its size, the niche was presumably designed to contain a single inhumation.

Inhumations

The tombs in both groups were clearly used for successive burials. The only exception is Tomb 10 which had six bodies systematically laid out on the floor of the chamber, indicating perhaps that they are contemporary (Plate 3). The bodies in the West Cemetery were not placed in coffins, and generally have no protection except for their wrappings, though cartonnage head and foot coverings were occasionally employed. The latest additions to the burial chambers were frequently placed on top of previous inhumations. Disarticulated and disturbed human remains were spread around the rear and sides of each chamber, apparently having been pushed aside to make room for later burials.

The treatment of the bodies and their positioning in the tomb varies between Group 1 and 2. The latest inhumations in Group 1 tombs were generally well-preserved mummified individuals placed with the feet towards the door of the chamber, that is along the axis of the tomb entrance passage. A substantial number of bodies in Group 1 tombs have been mummified: an example is Tomb 2 which contained 42 burials, 15 of which had been mummified.

In the tombs of Group 2, the latest inhumations were skeletons, with disturbed mummified remains located at the rear of the chamber or pushed to the sides. The bodies were almost invariably placed at right angles to the axis of the tomb, with the head to the west (Plate 4). They were simply wrapped and were frequently placed on small

Michael Birrell

Plate 3 West Cemetery: Tomb 10.

Plate 4 West Cemetery: Tomb 8 Bodies 1 and 2.

sandstone blocks or large pottery sherds (Plate 3). Tomb 3 contained 31 skeletons, the majority of which were disarticulated. Two of the bodies were wrapped and provided with painted cartonnage masks which have been dated on stylistic grounds to the Ptolemaic period.

In March 1992, five of the mummies from Tomb 5 and one from Tomb 6 were analysed by M. Cook, C. A. Marlow and P. Sheldrick. Autopsies were performed by opening the chest and abdominal cavities. Evidence of internal organs such as heart, lung, diaphragm, bowel, stomach, kidney and bladder were found in a very desiccated condition. The expedition had the use of a portable x-ray machine plus the radiological facilities of the Mut hospital for developing films. Further autopsies and examinations were undertaken in November 1992 by M. Zimmerman. In November–December 1993 A. Aufderheide, M. Zlonis and L. Cartmell performed autopsies on 15 mummified individuals. The thoracic and abdominal cavities were entered by removal of the ventral walls. The viscera were removed and samples of soft tissue were taken from each body for analysis. Skulls were examined by E. Molto. On completion of the autopsies, remaining soft tissue and skeletons were reburied.

The examinations revealed that some of the bodies had apparently desiccated in the tomb, since they had not been eviscerated and the internal organs were found intact. The best preserved bodies had all been treated with a black resin applied either to the body surface or to the linen wrappings. Resin was also frequently detected in the body cavities. The cranial cavity of each mummified body had been pierced by a trans-nasal craniotomy through the ethmoid bone, with resin applied to the inside of the skull. In such cases, the resin collected in the posterior of the cranium. The nostrils were normally plugged with wads of resin-soaked linen. Resin was also found in the thoracic cavity having entered either via the mouth and trachea or an opening into the pleural cavity. In several other bodies, the trunk cavities had been eviscerated via an abdominal incision and resin and resin-soaked linen was introduced into these cavities.

A few poorly preserved bodies had been stabilized and reconstituted with palm ribs which had been inserted down the spinal column (Tomb 8, Body 5; Tomb 12, Body 1). The projecting end of the stick, normally 1–1.5 cm in diameter, was wrapped in linen and passed up through the foramen magnum into the skull. Other poorly preserved bodies were tied to palm-rib racks. The racks were made from long pieces of rib bound to short lateral rods with palm-fibre twine or cloth.[3] An autopsy on Body P from Tomb 2, found tied to one of these racks, revealed that the remains consisted of parts from four different individuals.[4]

Loose racks, not associated with a particular body, were also found in Tombs 2, 3, 4 and 7.

Wooden rods were also used to maintain the form of skeletons. Body 2 in Tomb 13 was that of a small child which had been carefully wrapped and decorated with a painted cartonnage mask (Plate 7). The skeleton had been consolidated by two pieces of unworked wood which were inserted into the cranium via the foramen magnum.

The cloth used for wrapping the mummified bodies of the West Cemetery varied in quality and quantity. The preservation of the material depended on the amount of black resinous material applied to the outer surface of the body. Where there was a large quantity of resin, the linen has concreted and almost impossible to remove. The wrapping on Body B from Tomb 3 will serve as an example. The first layer of cloth was wrapped around the body and right arm leaving the left arm free. The entire body was then wrapped in a linen sheet which was held in place by a large quantity of linen bandaging. Over this layer, the body was wrapped in three pieces of fringed cloth which were doubled over the body. The ends of the cloth were folded over the feet so that the frayed ends rested against the shins. A circular linen wad had been placed under the head and was wrapped up with the cloth. The entire body was then wrapped in numerous layers of linen bandage (7–8 cm wide) which covered the entire body and the head. A separate, short linen bandage was tied around the neck as the final wrapping.

Poorly preserved bodies from Group 2 tombs (such as Tomb 8 body 1) had linen wadding around the abdomen and over the legs. This was covered with short pieces of coarse cloth and successive sheets of finer quality linen tied down with short lengths of bandage. The body was then covered with a red linen shawl which extended from neck to knee, affixed around the neck with a short linen bandage.

Tomb 5 contained the disturbed remains of two mummified bodies which retained a layer of gold foil applied directly to the skin of the hands, arms and face. Both bodies were disarticulated, presumably as a result of attempts to remove the gold.

Brief description of tomb contents

All of the tombs in the West Cemetery had been disturbed at some time prior to excavation. Nearly every tomb contained painted and gilded cartonnage in fragments on the tomb floor or in the sand fill of the entrance. The best preserved cartonnage was found in Tomb 10. A painted –

---

[3] Similar palm-rib racks were found at Dush, for which see F. Dunand, J-L. Heim, N. Henein, and R. Lichtenberg, *Douch 1: La nécropole*, Cairo, 1992, 226.

[4] Similar composite bodies of the Ptolemaic and Roman periods are described in G. E. Smith and F. W. Jones, *The Archaeological Survey of Nubia 1907–1908, volume II: Report on the Human Remains*, Cairo, 1910, 213–15.

Michael Birrell

Plate 5 West Cemetery: Tomb 10 Body 1.   *Plate 6 West Cemetery: Tomb 10 Body 1.*

Plate 7 West Cemetery: Tomb 13 Bodies 2 and 3.

Plate 8 West Cemetery: Tomb 13 Body 3.

Plate 9 West Cemetery: Tomb 13 ceramics.

and gilded-head and chest cover, and a foot cover were found *in situ* on Body 1 (Plates 5 and 6). The cartonnage comprises a coarse linen coated with white plaster. A layer of thick gilding and painted decoration had been applied to the outer surface. The depictions on the head covering include seated deities before offering stands, hawk heads mounted by solar disks, and sphinxes with mummiform figures on their back. The sphinxes have been identified by Olaf Kaper as representations of the god Tutu, the principal deity of the Main Temple of Kellis.

Painted cartonnage head covers were also found on Bodies 2 and 3 in Tomb 13 (Plate 7). The well-preserved example on Body 3 (Plate 8) has elaborate painted decoration and an applied stucco wreath, as do the other examples from the cemetery; over its feet was a fragmentary cover. Painted-cartonnage foot covers, decorated with scenes of *ba*-birds and seated deities, were found also in Tombs 3, 4 and 8. These had been disturbed and could not be associated with particular bodies.

A number of tombs contained painted wooden statues. A painted wooden *ba*-bird in Tomb 1 was found in the south-eastern corner of the chamber. A canine-headed figure, possibly to be identified as Anubis, was found in Tomb 5, and another was found in Tomb 6 against the northern wall. Two gilded and painted *ba*-birds were found in Tomb 10. The first represents the *ba*-bird with outstretched wings. A piece of linen bandaging passed between the feet and tail of the bird presumably to attach it to a body. It was found on Body 5 with the right wing broken. The second *ba*-bird was found on the floor of the tomb beside Body 5, with the head facing south. It had two slots for the insertion of wings, which were missing.

Two small sandstone offering tables were found in the entrance passage of Tomb 5 and another was located within the doorway of the tomb near the south wall. The first table has the representation of four loaves of bread on the upper surface. The second depicts five loaves of bread, a one-handled spouted jug and a jar with flaring neck. The third table depicts two spouted libation vessels and two circular loaves of bread.

Four of the tombs in the West Cemetery contained pottery (Tombs 1, 2, 9 and 13; see Patten, herein). A spouted jug with two handles (Patten, herein Figure 3.36) was found outside Tomb 1 in the sand fill of the entrance passage. A large jar was also found in the entrance passage of Tomb 9 (Patten, herein Figure 3.37). A simple spouted lamp and a small jar (Patten, herein Figure 3.35) were found in the sand fill within Tomb 2. Tomb 13 contained four vessels and a small woven fibre basket. Two small jars, one of which had horizontal bands of painted decoration, retained their clay seals wrapped in linen. The jar with the horizontal bands (Patten, herein Figure 3.32) was found on the chest of Body 1, the other jar (Patten,

herein Figure 3.33) was resting against the north wall and a shallow bowl (Patten, herein Figure 3.29) lay in the centre of the tomb (Plate 9). A third jar (Patten, herein Figure 3.34), coated with black resinous material, was found against the east wall beside the woven basket.

Each tomb contained miscellaneous botanical remains, with small bouquets of rosemary found in Tombs 3, 4 and 15.

Preliminary study of the objects from the tombs in the West Cemetery suggests that it was in use from the Ptolemaic period into the early Roman period. The ceramics and cartonnage from Tomb 13 have been assigned to the Ptolemaic period, the cartonnage on Tomb 10 Body 1 has been dated to the first century CE and the spouted jug from near the entrance to Tomb 1 to the first-second centuries CE. The large jar from Tomb 9 predates the late third century CE and may be as early as the Ptolemaic period.[5]

The East Cemetery (31/420–C5–2)

The East Cemetery is located on a low undulating rise approximately 200 m north-east of the northernmost mud-brick mausolea in the North Tomb Group (Hope 1988, 161–2; Winlock 1936, 21, Plates XI–XII). The cemetery occupies a plateau which is three metres above the base of the main *wadi* and is separated from the northern end of the North Tomb Group by a deep dry rivulet. The surface of the plateau is covered with wind-blown sand, flints and limestone pebbles, pottery sherds and bleached human bones. Mud-brick enclosure walls, low mud-brick superstructures and grave pits are clearly visible. The cemetery extends for at least 150 m east-west and 60 m north-south. It is densely filled with pit graves cut into the red Nubian clay. The surface has been subjected to wind erosion, causing many of the grave mouths to be exposed. The pits ordinarily contain single inhumations, the bodies placed supine with the head on the west.

The February 1991 examination of the area by P. Sheldrick was designed to determine the nature of the cemetery. Test excavations were begun at the north-west corner of the rise. Systematic excavation took place in November 1992, when he began clearing a 10 m by 10 m area at the western edge of the site. This region is dominated by two mud-brick enclosures containing pit graves with mud-brick superstructures. These are surrounded by isolated graves with superstructures and a great number of simple pit graves. During November–December 1993, 19 pit graves were excavated by the writer and P. Sheldrick in a 10 m by 10 m square north of the enclosures. A total of 56 graves have been excavated to date (Figure 3).

---

[5] (Eds) This assesment of the dating has been provided by C. A. Hope; information concerning the suggested dating of the cartonnage from the tombs derives from Annie Schweitzer in personal communication to C. A. Hope (September 1998), and of the ceramics from P. F. French and S. F. Patten (1998, personal communication, July).

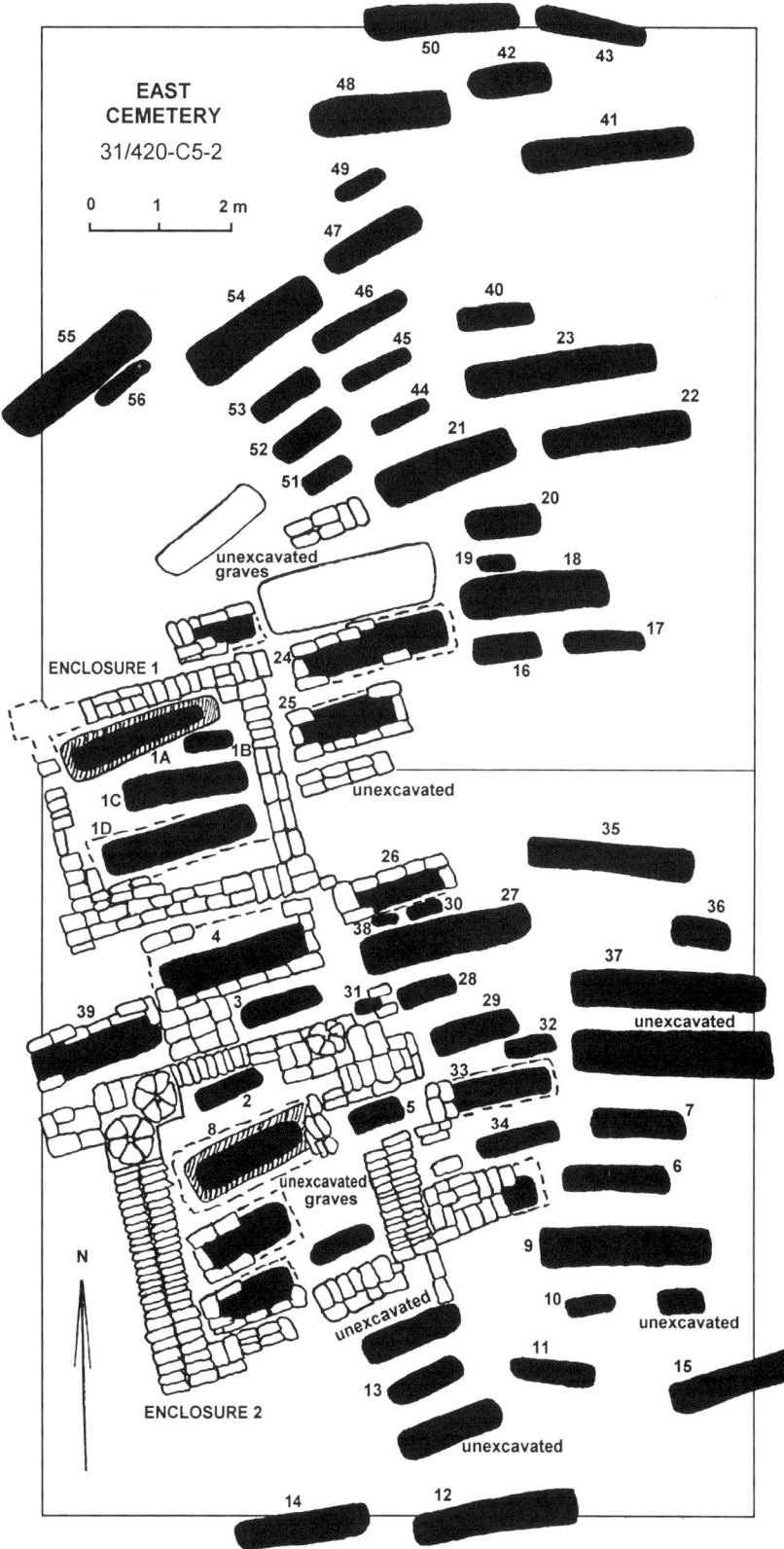

Figure 3 Plan of the excavated section of the East Cemetery.

Plate 10 East Cemetery: Grave 55.

Enclosure 1 is a small walled area containing graves with mud-brick superstructures. The walls of the enclosure are preserved to a maximum of three courses. Each corner of the structure is buttressed with additional bricks, and the external dimensions are 338 cm north-south by 337 cm east-west. The exterior and interior surfaces of the walls, as well as the floor of the enclosure, were covered with a coarse white gypsum plaster. A limestone door pivot found in the enclosure indicates that there may have been a door, but there is no other evidence of its existence. Four graves are located within the enclosure; three of adults and one of a child. All bodies were supine and oriented east-west with the heads to the west. The southernmost grave (1D) was the most elaborate and contained the skeleton of an adult female. The pit was lined with mud bricks placed on their edges. These supported a vault of mud bricks over the body. A mud-brick superstructure, preserved to a height of 60 cm, was erected on the surface.

Enclosure 2 is located two metres to the south of Enclosure 1 and consists of a walled area of approximately four square metres surrounding five graves with mud-brick superstructures. Two infants' graves (2 and 5) are intrusive in the north and east sides. The walls of the enclosure have been badly effected by wind erosion and are preserved to a maximum of two courses. There are traces of mud-brick columns, 60 cm in diameter and composed of wedge-shaped bricks, two at the north-west and one at the north-east corners. There is no indication of columns at the corners of the southern end. The most elaborate grave in the enclosure is Grave 8, which contained an adult female. The superstructure had external dimensions of 230 cm by 86 cm and was preserved to a height of 16 cm (1.5 courses). The sides of this mud-brick mastaba were covered with unpainted mud plaster. The mouth of the pit was 190 cm by 60 cm, and the depth was 133 cm. The lowest 35 cm of the pit were cut at a smaller size (160 cm by 40 cm) producing a ledge around the entire inner surface. Mud-bricks formed a vault resting on the lip of this ledge. The interior of the lowest part of the grave and the top of the gable was lined with straw-tempered mud plaster.

The two mud-brick enclosures are surrounded on all sides by pit graves surmounted by simple mud-brick superstructures. A large grave placed between the two enclosures (Grave 4) consisted of a mound of sand and gravel covered by a single layer of mud bricks coated with white gypsum plaster.

The graves located at a greater distance from the two enclosures have no superstructures but are simple pits cut into the red Nubian clay. These pits vary in length, width and depth depending on the size of the skeleton interred. Children were buried in very shallow graves, and as a result have been exposed by wind erosion. Some infants or foetuses were buried in close proximity to adult graves, and in one instance were buried in shallow pits under the sides of the mud-brick superstructure which covered the adult: Graves 30 and 38 are located under the brick covering of Grave 26.

Each grave had a single inhumation which was placed on the hard clay at the bottom of the pit. No coffins were used. The bodies have all been reduced to skeletons by the action of ground water, but they are generally undisturbed. The hands were placed over the pubic region or beside the thighs; in the majority of the burials of females the former position was usual.

The bodies in the East Cemetery were simply wrapped in linen cloth which usually does not survive apart from loose rags around the feet of adult skeletons. Some of the infant wrappings are better preserved. Grave 56 contained a wrapped infant with some soft tissue remaining on the lower part of the torso and around the legs. A coarse weave cloth had been placed under the body and folded over. The infant had then been placed on a second cloth of finer weave which was folded over the body with the excess cloth doubled back under the head. Fine linen cord was used to bind the wrappings.

Few of the graves contained artefacts. None of the bodies were decorated with jewellery or amulets. Grave 24 contained the supine skeleton of an adult female. A rectangular green glass bottle had been placed over the right shoulder. Its form suggests a date of manufacture in the second century CE (Marchini, herein). Some of the pits contained loose pottery sherds placed over or near the face of deceased infants. In other instances, the entire grave was covered with pottery. The most distinctive ceramic type from the East Cemetery is the so-called pigeon pot (Patten, herein Figure 3.38; also Hope 1979, 190, Plate XIX.11)). In Grave 55, belonging to an adult female, large fragments from three pigeon pots and a large painted jar covered the torso and legs of the body (Plate 10). The lower section of a fifth vessel was placed upright, covering the face of the deceased. The ceramic evidence indicates that this cemetery was only in use during the fourth century CE.

The Coinage: A Preliminary Report

Gillian E. Bowen

Excavations at Ismant el-Kharab conducted during the 1993 season yielded 174 coins, 123 of which were found in House 4, 41 in the West Church, four in the Main Temple, one in Shrine I and the remaining five were surface finds. This brings the total number of coins discovered thus far to 419. Most were heavily corroded and cleaning was undertaken by the conservator, Michelle Berry, who was assisted during the 1993 season by Paul Hunt. The majority of coins are small denomination bronzes dating to the fourth century CE.

Date Range

The period of occupation at the site has yet to be determined although current evidence suggests that it spans the first to the late fourth centuries at which time it appears to have been abandoned.[1] The coinage confirms this evidence. The earliest coins identified date to the reign of Hadrian, 117–138, and the latest to a type which was struck between 388 and 395.

The Main Temple

Coins found within the Main Temple range in date from year four of Hadrian, 119–120, to the *Spes Reipublicae* series of Julian II as Caesar, 335–361. Two of the small mud-brick chambers which lie to the south of the South Corridor, and are late additions to the temple complex, yielded two coins of Diocletian and one of Maximian dated between 284–296. Two of the coins were found in floor deposits and the third was within the floor itself. As the coins are pre-reform issues it would be unlikely, though by no means impossible, for them to have been in circulation for many years after their striking. The excellent condition of two of the specimens lends weight to this

supposition and one is led to conclude that their loss occurred not many years after the currency reforms of 296 at the latest. The construction of the small chambers must have taken place before that time.

Shrine I

A solitary coin found above the stable deposits which overlie the floor in Shrine I was struck under Crispus, 317–326.

House 3

Two hundred and eight coins, which include eight fragments, were excavated in House 3; 110 have been identified with confidence and a further nine have been given tentative ascriptions. The distribution is such that large numbers of coins were concentrated in five of the 13 rooms. Whether the presence of the coins is due to loss as a result of carelessness, their low value, or whether some represent scattered hoards cannot be ascertained. The coins range in date from Antoninus Pius, 138–161, to a *Salus Reipublicae* issue struck between 388–395. The data relating to the distribution within the house and the identification of the issues are presented in tabular form below.

It should be emphasized that the coins were retrieved from a well-defined archaeological context in floor deposits relating to the last phase of occupation, a context which is unlikely to have suffered any post-abandonment contamination (Hope et al. 1989, 3–4; 1992, 41–2). As only 56% of the coins from House 3 are identifiable, any conclusions relating to the abandonment of the premises based upon numismatic evidence must take into consideration the possibility that the sample is not truly representa-

---

[1] For the date range of activity attested by the Greek documents see Worp 1995; for a general survey of the evidence see Hope, in press a.

House 3: Distribution, identification and summary.

Distribution:

Room 2	60	Room 5	3	Room 9	48
Room 3	5	Room 6	2	Room 10	23
Room 4	22	Room 8	45		

Identification by room:

Room 2	*Deposit 3*			*Deposit 4*			*Deposit 5*	
	Antoninus Pius	1		Constantine I	1		Constantius II	3
	Constantius II	6		Constantius II	10			
	Julian II	3		Julian II	2		*Deposit 6*	
	Valentinian I /						Constantius II	1
	Valens	3						
Room 3	*Deposit 3*							
	Valentinian II?	1						
Room 4	*Deposit 3*			*Deposit 4*				
	Constantius II	6		3rd century	1		Constantine I	2
				Diocletian	1		Constantine II	
							Caesar	1
Room 5	*Deposit 4*			*Deposit 5*				
	Constantine I	1		Constantine I	1			
Room 6	*Deposit 4*							
	Crispus	1						
	Constantius II	1						
Room 8	*Deposit 3*			*Deposit 4*				
	Constantius II	1		Constantine I	10		Constantius II	14
	Julian II	1		Constantine II Caesar	3		Helena	1
				Constans	1		Valens	3
Room 9	*Deposit 3*			*Deposit 4*			*Deposit 5*	
	Constantius II	9		Constantine I	1		Constantius II	2
	Julian II	1		Constantius II	4			
				Julian II	1			
Room 10	*Deposit 3*			*Deposit 3 on 4*				
	Constantius II	8		Numerian	1		Constantius II	5
	Julian II	1		Constantine II Caesar	2		Constantine I	2
				Constans Caesar	1		(posthumous	
				Constantius II Caesar	1		issue)	

Summary by reign:

Antoninus Pius	1	138–61	Helena	1	337–40
third century	1		Constantine I	2	337–40
Numerian	1	283–84	(posthumous issue)		
Diocletian	1	284–96	Constantius II	70	337–61
Constantine I	16	307–37	Julian II	9	361–63
Crispus	1	317–26	Valentinian I/		
Constantine II Caesar	6	317–37	Valens	6	364–78
Constans Caesar	1	333–37	Valentinian II?	1	388–95
Constantius II Caesar	1	324–37			
Constans	1	337–50			

tive of the whole. One second-century drachma of Antoninus Pius is worthy of discussion. The coin was found within the same context as those of Constantine I and Constantius II and it is probable that its loss occurred during the latter half of the fourth century. The coin is extremely worn, testimony itself to its longevity within the currency pool. There are two possible explanations for its presence: either it is a stray, or, as the coin is a multiple of AE2 fourth-century issues, it could have continued to function as legal tender in the currency pool. Stray survivor coins from imperial times are attested in all parts of the Roman world; some are known to have been in circulation for well over one hundred years after their date of issue. The presence of a coin dating to the years 388–95 and the absence of any issues from the fifth century argues for an abandonment sometime during the last decade of the fourth century, a date which is compatible with the papyrological documentation (Worp 1995, no. 26).

House 4

During the 1993 excavation season House 4 yielded 123 coins. The coins were heavily oxidized and only 37 could be identified and dated with certainty, although a further 3 can be assigned to specific emperors with a degree of confidence. All coins retrieved were single finds and the date range approximates that of House 3 with the earliest specimen being from the first half of the second century, probably Hadrian, 117–138, and the latest being those struck by Valens, 364–78.

As with the specimens from House 3, the Hadrian issue is extremely worn which suggests another survivor. The poor state of preservation of the coins has rendered only 30% identifiable, too few to allow any conclusions to be drawn. If the structure continues to yield coins in the quantities that it has thus far then a clearer picture, not only of the date of abandonment of the house but also of its occupational span, should emerge.

House 4: Distribution, identification and summary.

Distribution:

Room 1A	5	Room 7A	3	Room 14	1
Room 3	7	Room 8	1	Room 24	2
Room 4	6	Room 9	1	Room 26	18
Room 5	2	Room 12	2	Room 27A	24
Room 6	48	Room 13	3		

Identification by room:

Room 1B	*Deposit 2*						
	Constantius II	1					
	Julian II	1					
Room 3	*Deposit 4*						
	Julian II	1					
Room 4	*Deposit 1a*		*Deposit 1*		*Deposit 3*		
	Valens	1	Constantius II	1	Constantine I (?)	1	
					Constantine II	1	
					Julian II	1	
Room 5	*Deposit 1*						
	Valens	1					
Room 6	*Deposit 1a*		*Deposit 7*		*Deposit 8*		
	Constantine I	1	Constantine I	6	Diocletian	1	
	Deposit 5		Constantius II	4			
	Constantius II		Constantius II (?)	1			
		1	Julian II	1			
Room 7A	*Deposit 3*						
	Constantine I	1					
	Constantius II	1					
Room 8	*Deposit 2*						
	Constantine I	1					
Room 9	*Deposit 2*						
	Constantius II	1					
Room 12	*Deposit 2*						
	Hadrian (?)	1					
	Constantine II Caesar						
		1					
Room 13	*Deposit 3*		*Deposit 4*				
	Julian II Caesar	1	Constantius II	1			

Room 24	*Deposit 3*		
	Constantius II	1	
	Constantius II (?)	1	
Room 26	*Deposit 3*		
	Diocletian (?)	1	
	Constantius II	2	
	Constantius II (?)	1	
Room 27A	*Deposit 4*		
	Constantius II	2	

Summary by reign:

Hadrian (?)	1	117–38	Constantine II	1	337–40
Diocletian	1	284–96	Constantius II	15	337–61
Diocletian (?)	1	pre-296	Constantius II (?)	3	337–61
Constantine I	9	307–37	Julian II Caesar	1	335–60
Constantine I (?)	1	307–37	Julian II	4	361–63
Constantine II Caesar	1	317–37	Valens	2	364–78

The West Church

The West Church yielded 41 coins, three of which were recovered from the church itself and the remaining 39 were from the adjoining structure. The coins are in a bad state of preservation and only 19 are identifiable, 12 of which can be dated with confidence. These range in date from Constans as Caesar, 333–337, to the reign of Valens, 364–378.

Only 46% of the coins from the West Church are identifiable, therefore, one must make allowances, yet again, for a possible distortion of the evidence. With this in mind, the specimens identified suggest a period of use from the mid- to late fourth century only.

The West Church: Distribution, identification and summary.

Distribution by room:

Narthex	2	Room 3	3	Room 6	14
Nave	1	Room 4	6	Room 7	10
Room 1	5				

Identification by room:

Room 1	*Deposit 7*						
	Valentinian I/						
	Valens	1					
Room 3	*Deposit 5*						
	Julian II	1					
Room 4	*Deposit 2 (low)*		*Deposit 5*				
	Constantius II	1	Constantius II	1			
Room 6	*Deposit 2 on 3*		*Deposit 4 on 5*		*Deposit 5*		
	Constantius II	1	Constantius II	1	Jovian	1	
			Julian II	1	Valentinian I/		
					Valens	3	
Room 7	*Deposit 2 on 3*		*Deposit 3*		*Deposit 4*		
	Constans Caesar	1	Julian II Caesar	1	Constantius II	1	
	Constantius II	2	Julian II	1			
	Valens	1	Valentinian II	1			

Summary by reign:

Constans Caesar	1	333–37	Jovian	1	363–64
Constantius II	7	337–61	Valentinian I/		
Julian Caesar	1	355–60	Valens	5	364–78
Julian II	3	361–63	Valentinian II	1	375–92

Denominations

A summary of the denominations of the fourth-century bronzes follows:

Denomination	Specimens	Weight	%
AE1	–	–	–
AE2	18	4.5g – 6.6g	4.8%
AE3	123	2.7g – 3.8g	32.8%
AE4	233	0.8g – 2.5g	62.3%

Mint Distribution

Prior to the reforms under Diocletian in 296, Egypt's currency was closed; only coinage struck in Alexandria was legal tender. Post-reform coinage, however, attests a wide circulation of currency from mints throughout the empire. An exposition of circulation patterns for coinage retrieved from Egyptian sites is urgently needed. An assessment of available evidence indicates that during the fourth century the mint at Alexandria struck only 35% of Egypt's requirements; an estimated 20% was supplied by the mint of Antioch, 35% from the eastern mints whilst the Roman mint accounted for almost 5% (Kent 1981, 95).

A positive mint identification has been possible for 86 of the fourth century coins retrieved from Kellis:

Alexandria	33
Antioch	19
Nicomedia	10
Constantinople	9
Rome	5
Thessalonika	3
Heraklea	2
Siscia	2
Arles	1
Lyons	1
Trier	1

It should be noted that this distribution reflects the pattern for Egypt in general. One is led to conclude that their presence is a result of trade, direct or indirect. The volume of coins retrieved confirms that Kellis participated in a cash economy and probably one of mobility; the variety of mints represented is indicative of the extent of the trade network and the currency circulation of the Roman world, a world in which Kellis participated fully.

Imitations

Two imitations have been identified amongst the coins. Their presence is not altogether unexpected as the practice of copying coins, usually small-denomination bronzes, was prevalent during the mid-fourth century and indeed became endemic in the West. Coin-finds from the excavations at Dush in the Kharga Oasis included several copies (Gautier 1981, 112) whilst an estimated quarter of those retrieved from the rubbish dumps at Oxyrhynchus were found to be imitations (Milne 1971, xv). The purpose for the manufacture of imitations is not entirely understood although it is generally assumed that it was necessitated by an insufficient supply of low-denomination coinage which was required to carry out minor transactions. The paucity of official coinage was further supplemented by lead tokens; one such token was found in House 4. What is surprising is that there are so few imitations represented in the sample, the absence of such warrants further investigation.

Concluding Remarks

The study of the coinage offers great potential for the dating of the occupation and final abandonment of the individual structures as well as the site as a whole. Moreover, the context in which the dated coins are found will allow a more precise chronology to be given to other categories of objects. The coins thus far examined, however, complement the evidence gleaned from the ceramic studies and from the dated textual material, none of which extends into the fifth century. Dating by use of coins is not without its problems and one must take into account the length of time that the coin was in the circulation-pool before its loss. The possibility of regional variations in relation to longevity of circulation should also be taken into consideration. As has been noted, coins of the first two centuries of this era remained in circulation for in excess of one hundred years; although the sample is limited, Kellis appears to reflect this pattern. The circulation life of coins can be ascertained, to a degree, by comparison with data derived from the study of hoards. Seriation, a method based upon the association of coins found together in a single context, can also be used to build a data bank which should provide more reliable evidence for the circulation-life of individual issues (Collis 1988, 198).

Progress on the Coptic Texts from Ismant el-Kharab

Iain Gardner

Excavations at Ismant el-Kharab in the residential quarter of Area A until 1992 recovered a considerable quantity of textual material from Houses 1–3 and the North Building (A/1–5), of which a good proportion is written in fourth century Coptic. In 1993 archaeological work, still in progress, moved to House 4 (A/6) where further Coptic texts of approximately the same date have already been found. This report will summarize editorial work on this material till May 1994 and direct the reader to more detailed studies already published elsewhere, or as projected.

During the 1993 and 1994 seasons A. Alcock and I. Gardner sorted and reconstructed the Coptic texts on site, while continuing editorial work by means of photographs during the off-season periods. A provisional listing suggests that from a much greater number of fragments approximately 150 discrete documents can be identified. Minor fragments and 'scraps' may increase this total. Of this, depending upon definition, perhaps 80 contain sufficient recoverable text or are of such specific interest as to warrant full publication at this time.

The material has been divided according to content. Literary (essentially religious) material is being edited by I. Gardner. Documentary (essentially personal letters and economic) material is being edited by a team consisting of A. Alcock, W.-P. Funk and I. Gardner (coordinator). However, it is apparent that both types belonged to the same communities, that is the residential inhabitants of Area A; and similarly the majority at least of the large Greek archive, of which the editorial work is being coordinated by K. Worp. Thus all papyrologists on the team work in close collaboration.

All of the Kellis texts are at present being prepared for publication in the official Dakhleh Oasis Project monograph series. The first volumes are projected to appear from 1995. These will include a first set of Coptic literary material prepared by I. Gardner, (at minimum those texts listed below under sections B, C and E); and of Greek documentary material prepared by K. Worp.[1]

Coptic Literary Texts

All such material is either Manichaean in content, or, as in the case of a single codex leaf from Paul's Epistle to the Romans, may at this time be reasonably supposed to have been used by members of a Manichaean community at Kellis. Comments and some provisional text editions can be found in: I. Gardner, "A Manichaean Liturgical Codex found at Kellis", *Orientalia* 62 (1993), 30–59; and *ibid*, "The Manichaean Community at Kellis: Progress Report", *Acta Orientalia Belgica* VIII (1993), 75–87 (and see also an abbreviated version in *Manichaean Studies Newsletter* 11 (1993), 18–26).

A. Canonical works by Mani

i. ex P93C[2] etc.

About 100 fragments from a papyrus codex containing canonical Epistle/s by Mani.

Substantial remains of perhaps nine leaves survive and are in the process on reconstruction. The well-attested opening for an epistle by Mani can be demonstrated:

[(I) Mani, The ap]ostle of [Je]su[s] Chrestos, a[nd] all the other bre[thren who are wi]th me ...

---

[1] (Eds) Since the above was written the following volumes have been published: K. A. Worp, *Greek Papyri from Kellis: I*, Oxford 1995; I. Gardner, *Kellis Literary Texts Volume 1*, Oxford, 1996; R. S. Bagnall, *The Kellis Agricultural Account Book*, Oxford, 1997; K. A. Worp and A. Rijksbaron, *The Kellis Isocrates Codex*, Oxford, 1997.

[2] Such references are to the papyrus deposit numbers which are assigned by the excavator.

The form 'Chrestos', i.e. Jesus the Good, is found throughout. Interestingly, Alexander of Lycopolis (*Critique of the doctrines of Manichaeus* 34:18–21) notes that the Manichaeans used this form; although there is little evidence for it in other texts.

ii.   ex P30/55/59B
Single papyrus codex leaf from an Epistle (?) by Mani, concerning *agape* and *sophia*.

B. Manichaean doctrinal texts
i.   A/5/346[3]
Catechetical text on wooden board concerning the five *schema* of the Father.

C. Manichaean psalms and liturgical texts
i.   A/5/53B
Manichaean liturgical codex on wooden boards, containing probably six psalms and an eschatological prayer (Gardner 1993). Text A2 is an abbreviated version of Medinet Madi psalm 68.

ii.   A/5/6
Two Manichaean psalms on wooden board. The first parallels Medinet Madi psalm 222, Allberry (1938) 8:6 to the end; the second is psalm 109, in Giversen's (1988) facsimile of the *Psalm Book* 1, pl. 154.

iii.   A/5/195
Poorly preserved Manichaean psalm/s on wooden board. Medinet Madi psalm 261 identified.

iv.   A/5/107
Small fragment wooden board, Manichaean psalm.

v.   A/6/14
Manichaean psalm/s on wooden board.

vi.   P82A
Manichaean psalms on papyri; text A parallels Medinet Madi psalm 246, Allberry (1938) 55:3–13, but does not include the doxology.

vii.   P82Bi/ii
Manichaean psalms on papyri. Includes a somewhat garbled version of a Medinet Madi psalm found in Giversen's (1988) facsimile of the *Psalm Book* 1, pl. 277–278.

viii.   P92.17A
Fragment of Manichaean psalm on papyrus.

There is in all at least eighteen psalms very similar in style and terminology to the Medinet Madi Psalm Book (Allberry 1938, and for facsimile editions of Parts I and

II, Giversen 1988). As yet six have been identified, and there seems little doubt that further parallels may be discovered, especially when Part I of the Chester Beatty codex is edited. From the textual evidence it seems certain that the Kellis versions predate those from Medinet Madi. The six identified come from widely divergent portions of the codex, and show no evidence of the numerical sequence established in the Medinet Madi codex. They equate to psalms 68, 109, 222, 246, 261, and one as yet unplaced.

A further point worthy of note is not so much the quantity of Coptic Manichaean psalms, but the variety of different hands, and the evidence of many codices both on wooden board and papyrus. A number of the hands are unpractised, while others are good, such on occasion appearing in conjunction. This requires explanation.

D. Coptic-Syriac glossaries of Manichaean technical terms
i.   A/5/196
Glossary of cosmological terms on wooden board.

ii.   A/5/239
Glossary of devotional terms, wooden board.

E. Biblical texts
i.   P75A
Single leaf of Coptic codex (dialect *I*), from Paul's Epistle to the Romans, chapter 2.

F. Miscellaneous literary fragments from Houses 2–3
i.   A/2/88
Poorly preserved codex leaf, probably Manichaean.

ii.   P27B
Literary fragments from a codex.

iii.   P82C
Page from a codex, mostly illegible.

Although the volume of this material is not great, compared to the Medinet Madi corpus, the variety and literary quality is impressive. The texts identified as by Mani are unique. However, it is possible that parallels may be found in the remaining and as yet unedited leaves from the Medinet Madi codex of the *Epistles*; W.-P. Funk and I. Gardner are at present editing these (to be published by Kohlhammer, Stuttgart). The psalms predate the Medinet Madi codex of the *Psalm-Book*. The passage from Paul's Epistle to the Romans, and a Greek text related to the *Acts*

---

[3] This type of reference provides the excavation object inventory number.

of John,[4] are to be regarded as having been used by the Manichaean community at Kellis, rather than as Christian. In particular, the bilingual Coptic/Syriac glossaries may seem to evidence the presence of a Manichaean missionary cell at Kellis, engaged in the actual process of translating the religion and its texts. As will be seen also from the personal letters, it seems certain that the community were not only lay believers (catechumens), but included the elect as well, the higher and professional grade of the church. These texts are also highly valuable for the study of early Coptic dialects and Manichaean Syriac; and for codicology, palaeography, and such disciplines.

Most of this material was found in House 3 (A/5). However, the psalm from House 4 (A/6/14) indicates clearly that this was not an isolated group of believers. If the text A/2/88 can be identified as Manichaean, then that would widen the evidence to House 2 as well. Indeed, there has been little unambiguously Christian material found yet at Kellis, and the relative strengths of the communities in the fourth century is open to debate. Here the future excavation of the churches at Kellis will be vital.

Documentary Texts

The extent of documentary texts is much greater. There are more Greek fragments than Coptic, but the number of useable texts in each language is perhaps approximately equal. The inhabitants of House 3 were bilingual and highly literate. There is as yet no evidence for supposing discrete periods of occupation, and some of the same inhabitants are referred to in both the Greek and Coptic documents. However, the languages appear largely to be used for different purposes. The Coptic texts are almost entirely personal letters, with only a few economic documents, and religious sentiment is often apparent. The Greek are predominantly economic and legal, with a lesser proportion of personal letters. These latter are mostly secular in purpose, though now characteristic Manichaean phraseology has been identified in one Greek personal letter (P87).

The team of A. Alcock, W.-P. Funk, and I. Gardner has now established a dossier of all the Coptic material, and systematic work has begun. It is envisaged that the text editions will be published in an ongoing series of volumes. Certainly the comments provided here must be accepted as highly provisional. The dossier of all Coptic documentary texts currently contains the following:

Houses 1–2 and the North Building (A/1–3): 8 files, 7 of which are from personal letters.

A/2/76+77 refers: r.6–7 'he went to the monastery with father Pebok'. 'The monastery' is also mentioned in P93.85+89 (from House 4). The Coptic word survives in the modern place-name of Teneida at the eastern extremity of the oasis.

A/1/173 is a wooden board with a Coptic syllabary on one side. There is a small portion of Syriac text, as yet unread, which may be the first evidence of Manichaeism in House 1. Some of the terminology in the letter A/3/32 may suggest a Manichaean author.

House 3 (A/5): 125 files.

A number of these refer only to small fragments that may be joined to others, thus reducing the total number; but then some files contain small fragments from two or more separate texts. Thus it is difficult to calculate exactly the total number of separate original documents recovered. However, it is likely to exceed 125 at the final count.

The material is almost entirely personal letters, although there are perhaps five economic texts such as receipts or personal accounts. Depending upon exact definition, there would seem to be the substantial remains of about 60–65 letters; that is, documents with more than a few lines of coherent text. A number are complete or virtually so. At present 21 separate letters have been marked as Manichaean (plus one Greek); that is, they contain distinctive terminology such as greeting someone as 'a good member of the Light Mind (a Manichaean divinity incarnate in the true church)'. However, it can be presumed, and the cross-referencing of authors will demonstrate this in the future, that a much greater percentage were actually written by Manichaean believers.

P80B+P92A is an economic account, with reference to the *agape* of Theodora (r.12).

House 4 (A/6): 4 files, with substantial remains of 3 personal letters; from the first season of excavation.

P93.89 is the most apparently Christian letter yet read. Interestingly its dialect is closer to Sahidic, while virtually all of the rest of the archive (especially from House 3) is uniformly written in Lycopolitan. The question of the perhaps socio-religious use of dialect is a matter that the team is beginning to debate.

P93.13A is a Latin text on which a Coptic invocation (?) has been written.

Clearly, there is extensive research to be undertaken before any definite conclusions can be presented. Many of the texts have only been cursorily read, and partially transcribed if at all. The process of reconstruction is not yet complete. However, for further comment see Gardner 1997.

---

[4] See now I. Gardner and K. A. Worp, 'Leaves from a Manichaean Codex', *Zeitschrift für Papyrologie und Epigraphik* 117 (1997), 139-55, and C. A. Hope, 'The Archaeological Context of the Discovery of Leaves from a Manichaean Codex', *Zeitschrift für Papyrologie und Epigraphik* 117 (1997), 156-61.

Interim Report on the West Tombs

Colin A. Hope and Judith McKenzie[1]

Excavations at Ismant el-Kharab between December 1992 and February 1993 (Bowen et al. 1993)[2] were again concentrated within the Main Temple of Tutu in Area D and the residential sector to their east, Area A.[3] In Area A a fourth house unit was selected for excavation, situated due east of the entrance into the outer temenos of the Main Temple. In the Main Temple complex parts of the court immediately west of the temple were investigated and work continued in Shrine I. In addition, within Area D work was inaugurated in the most northerly of the three enclosures which abut the north side of the enclosure containing the Main Temple. Here, excavation revealed a small two-roomed, fourth-century church (the West Church) with an eight-roomed, adjacent structure, and, immediately to their east, the remains of two tombs, termed the West Tombs. While the 1993–4 season saw little in the way of excavation,[4] study of the material from the previous season continued and it was possible to examine in detail the objects discovered in the West Tombs. This report will present a preliminary assessment of these two structures.

The Excavation and Tomb Contents

On the north side of the Main Temple enclosure (Enclosure 1) are located three other mud-brick enclosures (2–4). Two of these abut the north wall of the temple enclosure: Enclosure 2 lies on the east and Enclosure 3 on the west. The fourth contains an area to the north of Enclosure 3 but does not communicate directly with that enclosure. Visible at surface level within Enclosure 4 were the following: the small West Church and its associated structure, located in its north-east corner (Bowen et al. 1993, 23–5, 27) and, immediately to their east, the remains of two badly eroded stone platforms. East of these could be seen the outlines of small mud-brick rooms built against the north wall of the enclosure.[5] From the dissimilarity in orientation of the remains of the stone structures to the walls of the enclosure, the church and its ancillary building, it would appear that the former originally stood in isolation.[6]

Other than for the Main Temple and West Temple, the

---

[1] The discussion of the architecture of the superstructure of Tomb 1 is largely the work of McKenzie. It relies upon the records of the excavation and discussions with the excavator (Hope) and is made without the benefit of first-hand examination of either the structure or of the architectural fragments. Hope has provided the discussion of the tomb chambers and their contents.

[2] The excavations were funded by a major grant from the Australian Research Council, administered by Monash University. Additional support was received in the form of a travel scholarship provided by Rosemary and Eric Cromby (Melbourne) to enable a senior student of the Department of Greek, Roman and Egyptian Studies at Monash University to participate in the excavations. For this the Dakhleh Oasis Project is most grateful.

[3] Previous reports on the excavations by the present writer and colleagues can be found in Bowen et al. 1993; Hope 1985, 1986, 1987, 1988, 1990, 1991; Hope et al. 1989, 1992.

[4] The season was made possible through funding received from the Egyptology Society of Victoria, private donations and a travel scholarship from Rosemary and Eric Cromby.

[5] For a plan of these enclosures see Hope 1986, fig. 1. For a discussion of the site based upon the architectural remains visible upon the surface and as a result of testing during the course of the survey of the site see Knudstad and Frey, in press.

[6] This was observed by J. E. Knudstad during the survey of the area.

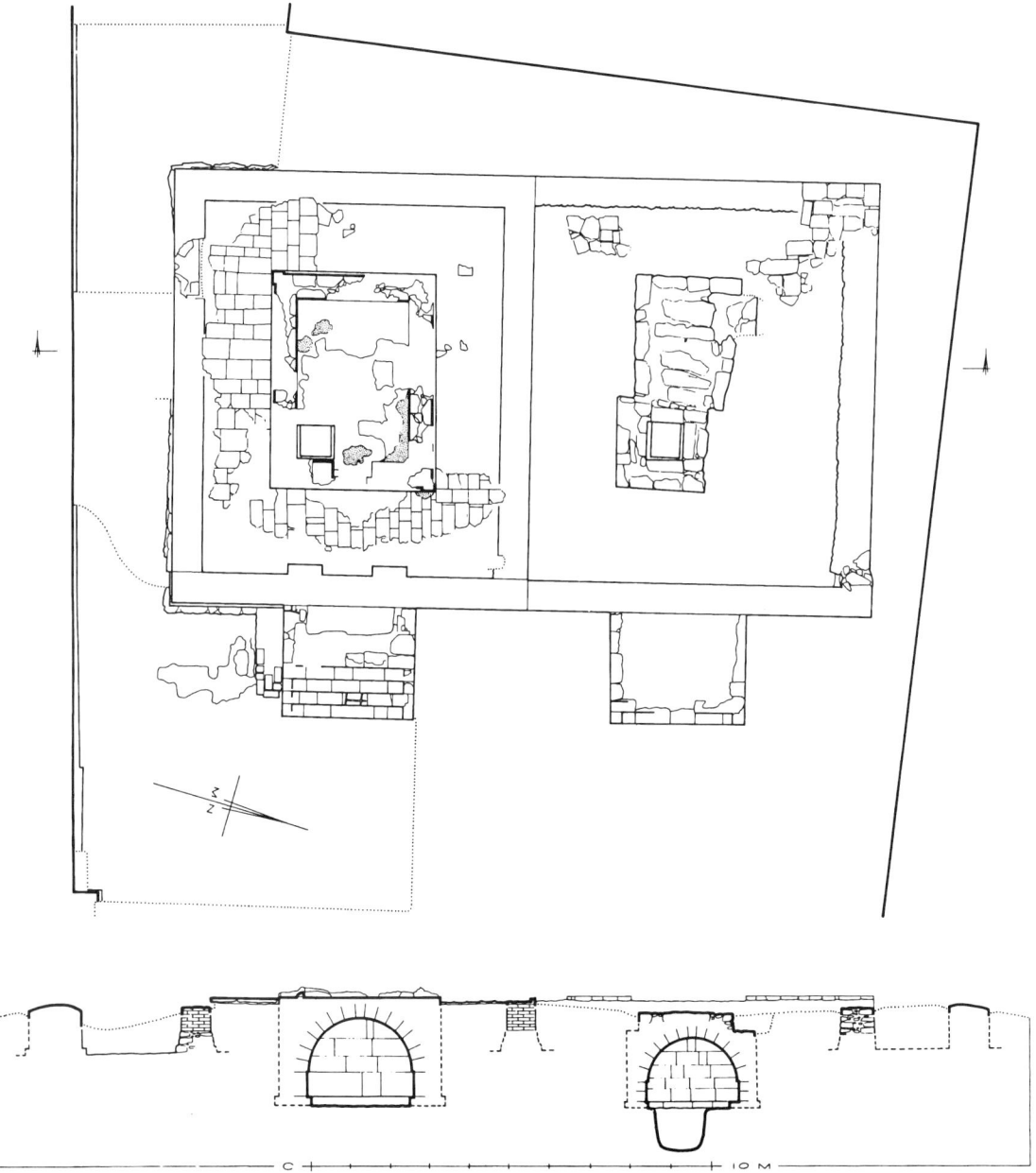

Figure 1 Plan and Section of the West Tombs (drawn by James E. Knudstad).

use of stone as a building material at Ismant el-Kharab appears to have been confined to the central chambers of two tombs in the North Tomb Group,[7] which are now poorly preserved, and the two structures in Enclosure 4. The examination of the latter was, therefore, imperative.

On clearance of surface sand the structures were seen to comprise the remains of two contiguous sandstone pavements set upon baked-brick platforms approached by flights of sandstone steps. At the centre of each was once

a single stone chamber; all trace of this chamber has disappeared in the case of the northern structure, which is in a poorer state of preservation than the southern one (Figure 1 and Plate 1). The southern tomb is labelled West Tomb 1 and the northern one West Tomb 2; the latter is built against the northern wall of the former, and therefore may post-date it.

Excavation around the platforms was restricted to an area east of the steps to Tomb 1, extending along its

[7] Tomb 1 here originally had painted reliefs applied to a plaster coating over the stone walls, see Winlock 1936, 21, pls XI–XII. The tomb chamber was actually cleared by B. Moritz who published an account of his work in 1900 in "Excursion aux Oasis du Désert Libyque", *Bulletin de la Societé Khédiviale de Géographie*, Ve Série No. 8, 449–75 (see pages 466–71). I am indebted to Olaf E. Kaper for this reference.

Plate 1 General view of the West Tombs and West Church, looking north-west.

southern side and to its south-west. This revealed fragments from a stone column and capitals, and a baked-brick capital, south-east of the tomb (Plate 10), and sections from baked-brick columns and a capital on its south and south-west (Plate 11). The fragments found to the south of the tomb derive from a single column, as do those from its south-west. Clearance of some surface sand on the west of the tomb revealed the existence of what may be three collapsed baked-brick columns there also. Thus the central chamber on the platform of Tomb 1, and presumably Tomb 2 also, would seem to have been surrounded by a peristyle colonnade. No remains of columns nor of the central chambers were found upon either platform, and it may be noted that no debris from the central chambers was discovered within the excavated area. This may indicate that they had been dismantled and the stone removed for reuse elsewhere, and that the columns had been pushed away from the structures during the course of dismantling. However, any fragments which remained or fell onto the platform could easily have disappeared through erosion by wind and sand if left exposed. This might then account for the fact that the remains of only one column were found from the south side of the tomb. The remains of the architecture of the superstructures is discussed below in more detail.

In the south-east corner of each of the central chambers

a stone-lined shaft gives access to a barrel-vaulted, stone-lined chamber. Each of these chambers has a rectangular recess at its north-east corner. The chamber of Tomb 2 was devoid of contents, other than a few human bones. Three pits had been dug into its floor, one at the base of the shaft, one in the recess and another in the south-eastern corner of the chamber. The clay from these pits was mounded into the chamber and held in place by a retaining wall roughly constructed from sandstone blocks and rubble. The dimensions of the floor of this tomb, including the shaft and recess, are 3.75 m east-west by 2.20 m north-south; the corners are not at right angles. It has a height of 1.90 m.

The situation in Tomb 1 was quite different. The burial chamber has a floor area, including shaft and recess, of 3.68–3.71 by 2.62–2.64 m and a height of 2.04 m. It is more carefully constructed than its neighbour, though no better finished. Here were found the remains of eleven interments, plus part of a possible twelfth,[8] upon the clay floor of the chamber, oriented approximately east-west; all but two (burials 1 and 11) had their heads on the east (Figure 2). Bodies 1–8 were immediately visible on the removal of sand which filled the shaft and the south-eastern corner of the chamber, while 9 and 10 were found under bodies 3 and 8, and 11 was found under 6. Bodies 7 and 8 lay partly under bodies 2 and 3, and their eastern

---

[8] The scant remains of this body were found with those of body 9.

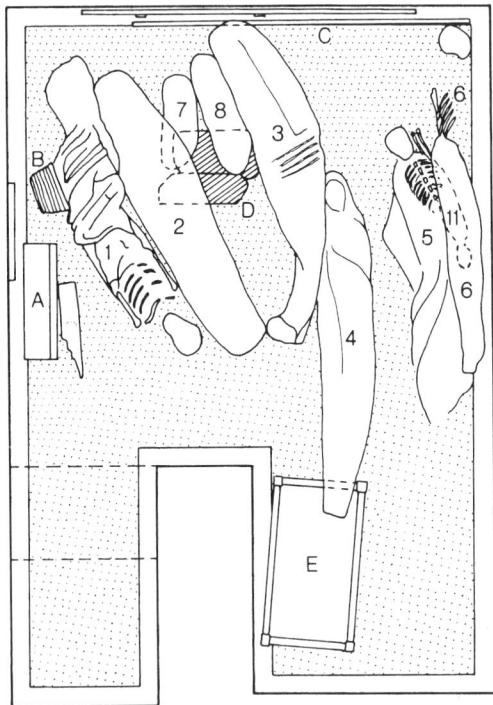

Figure 2 Plan of the burial chamber of West Tomb 1 showing location of interments 1–8 and 11, and contents. Scale 1:40

A   wooden pulley
B   woven, fibre basket
C   two sections from wooden board
D   two sandstone blocks;
E   bed.

Bodies 1–4 and 6 are those of adults, while 5 and 7–12 are those of juveniles. The impression created is that of a simultaneous, extended family burial. However, any such identifications must await the detailed examination of the remains by the team of physical anthropologists currently studying the human remains from the cemeteries of Ismant el-Kharab.[9]

The adults were well wrapped. Body 1 had at least 30 layers of wrappings and appears to have been covered with a shawl, as were the feet of body 3. Body 2 had a lozenge design created over the outer wrappings with thin strips of linen and may have been laid within a large linen sack. The quality of linen used varies, but some is extremely well woven and fine with fringed edges. The chest and abdomen regions of several of the bodies contained dark brown, hardened sand, which would appear to represent deliberate packing. Other evidence for mummification of the bodies must again await the detailed study of the remains.

Accompanying these burials were various objects. Against the southern wall of the tomb was part of a wooden pulley, 63.0 by 26.0 by 15.5 cm, (Figure 2.A, Plate 4), and against the western wall stood a wooden stretcher in fragments, 183.5 by 48.0 by 1.5 cm (Figure 2.C, Plate 2). Both of these items may have been used for lowering the bodies into the tomb. Also against the southern wall, and west of the pulley section, was a woven fibre basket (Figure 2.B, Plates 1b and 5) and in the recess was a small bed (Plate 3). The latter consists of a wooden frame with a woven fibre base; it measures 92.0 by 54.0 by 53.0 cm and is of the same design as examples found in Houses 1 and 2 in Area A of the site (Hope 1985, 118, Plates Va–b and 1987, 163). Thirty-five bouquets were distributed mainly around the edges of the chamber, with a concentration in the recess. One of these has been identified as comprising rosemary twigs with myrtle leaves (Thanheiser, herein). Accompanying the burials of bodies 5 and 6 were two pillows made of leaves wrapped in linen.

Ceramics were not abundant (Plate 6). A bowl (Plate 6, second row, centre) was found under the feet of body 1 and a blackened jar (Plate 6, rear left) under body 8. A small bowl which had been used to cover the mouth of a jar and which had been held in place by plaster (Plate 6 front) was found in the south-western corner. Fragments found at various places derive from another jar and two bowls (Plate 6, rear right, and centre row, left and right). Several glass vessels had been interred with these burials. Under body 8

ends lay over the most westerly of two sandstone blocks. While the location of these blocks may be thought unusual, a similar placement has been noted in tombs excavated within the cemetery to the west of Ismant el-Kharab (31/ 420–C5–1) and which was used by its inhabitants (Birrell, herein).

The interments were in a fragile condition. This was partly the result of the activity of robbers who had rifled several of the bodies (Plate 2) and disturbed their original placement, most apparent in the case of body 4 whose legs had been raised to rest upon the edge of a small bed situated within the recess (Figure 2 and Plate 3). However, much damage has also been caused by the action of salts, especially in the north-western corner of the chamber, both to the bodies and the tomb walls.

[9] Examination of these bodies subsequently has yielded the following identifications: body 1 is that of a female approximately 40 years at death, body 2 another female approximately 28 years at death, body 3 is that of a male approximately 25 years at death, body 4 another male of about 30–35 years at death, body 6 is possibly that of a male aged 22 years, and the remainder, whose sexes could not be determined, were aged 5–8 years at death. Several of the sub-adults were found to have been anemic; body 4 displayed evidence of arthritis in the neck and body 1 the same in the knees, body 3 had suffered a fractured left humerous, while body 2 may have died as a result of acute infection of the frontal sinus. The two adult females had both borne children. The adults were taller than the average of those found buried in the other cemeteries at the site. I am most grateful to P. Sheldrick and E. Molto for their analysis of these bodies.

Plate 2 West Tomb 1: burial chamber, general view of interments looking west.

Plate 3 West Tomb 1: burial chamber, showing legs of body 4 on bed in recess.

Plate 4: West Tomb 1: wooden pulley.

Plate 5 West Tomb 1: woven basket.

Plate 6 West Tomb 1: ceramics from the burial chamber.

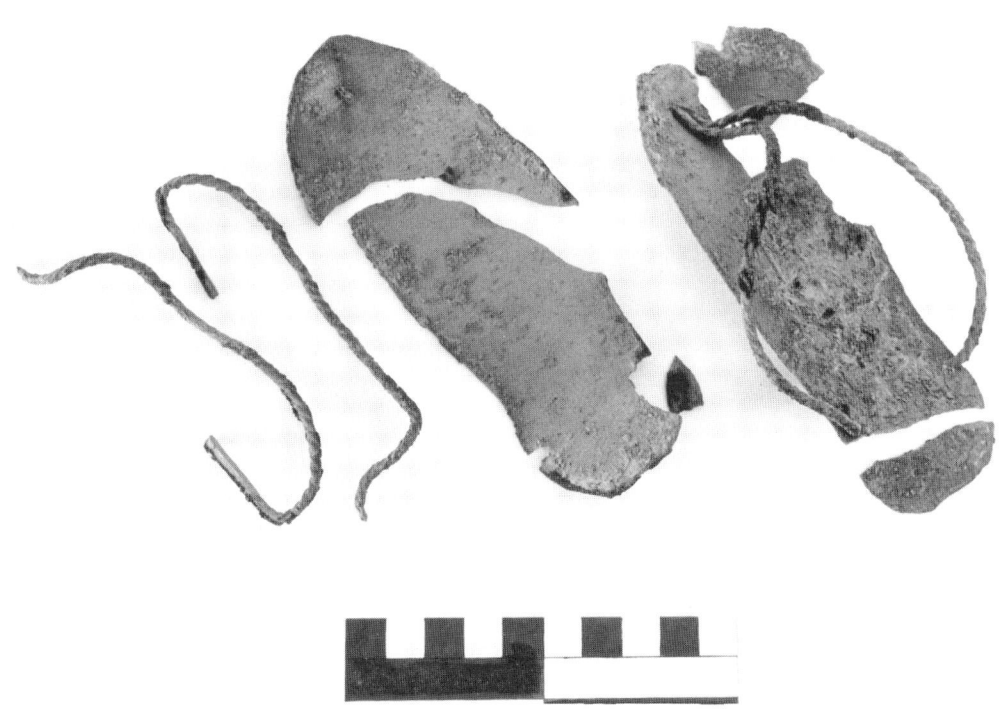

Plate 7 West Tomb 1: miniature lead sandals.

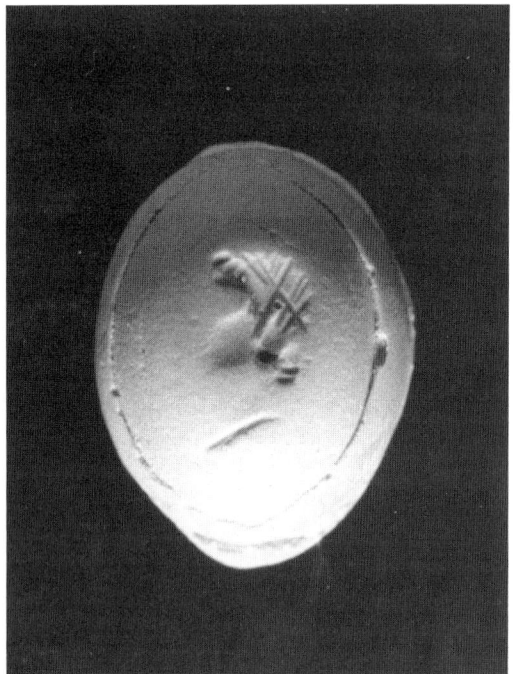

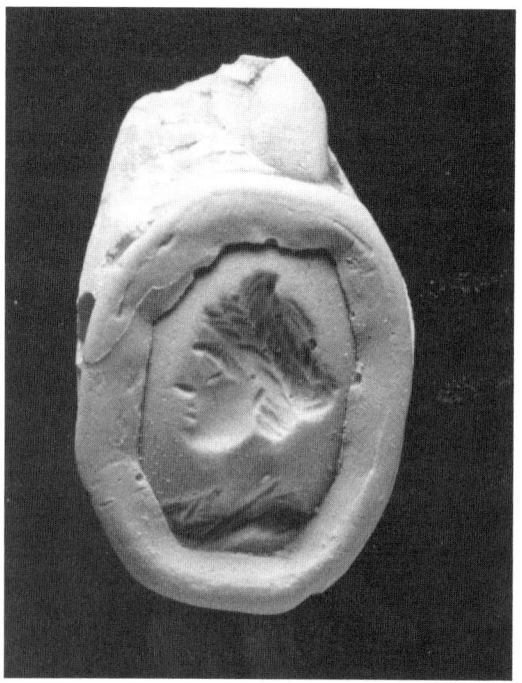

Plate 8 West Tomb 1: agate ring from body 3   *Plate 9 West Tomb 1: carnelian ring from body 3*

was found an intact vessel identified as an *ungentarium* or *lacrimarium*, near to which were fragments from a flask (Marchini, herein Figures 4b and 4c respectively). Sherds from the latter were found also under bodies 1 and 7. Fragments from three bowls/beakers were found in various locations (Marchini, herein Figures 4d–f).

A single amber bead was found under body 1. A finely-worked, silver cosmetic implement with a long, narrow shaft and a spatula-shaped end was found in several pieces in the fill of the tomb. Upon the footing of the north wall, due east of body 6, lay a pair of miniature lead sandals (Plate 7); one is damaged and the other measures 12.8 cm by a maximum of 5.2 cm. The soles are each made from a single piece, 0.1 cm thick; they have two straps attached by means of perforations at the front edge and at the side of the heel, and which were once soldered in place.

Other items of value comprise six gold finger rings. Three were found with body 3, the 25 year-old male, two with body 2, the 28 year-old female, and one against the north wall of the recess. The latter is a double ring, supporting small, blue glass stones; from body 2 one is a setting of a high-domed, oval agate and the other lacks its stone. These rings had been placed upon the right hand of the body. Of the three rings from body 3 one also lacks its stone. The remaining two consist of intact gems in their settings. One (Plate 8) is an oval agate preserving part of

a bust of a female (see below) in a much worn bezel. The other setting contains a carnelian cut with a finely executed bust of a female with elaborately braided hair (Plate 9). The mount is not original. Parallels to the hair style indicate a date within the Hadrianic Period (see below).

The ceramics, glass and rings from the tomb provide some indication of the date of the burials. The glass has been ascribed to the third century by Marchini (herein). The ceramic vessels resemble in general the shape, fabric and decoration of material excavated within a fourth century context in the houses of Area A. However, the details of the handled jar (Plate 6, rear right) might indicate a slightly earlier date for this piece, and all of the others could be ascribed equally to the second half of the third century as well as to the fourth. They do not resemble material of the second or early third century which has been excavated beneath the houses of Area A and in the Colonnaded Hall of Structure 1 in Area B (Patten, herein and Hope 1987, Figure 5, respectively).

The finger rings may confirm this dating. The mounts of the three rings from body 1 have tentatively been assigned a date from the third to fourth centuries (C. Johns, 1998, personal communication), although the two surviving gems appear to be earlier. I cite the comments of Donald Bailey (1998, personal communication)[10] concerning these two:

---

[10] I am indebted to Donald Bailey and Catherine Johns for their comments, which are based upon photographs and colour transparencies and not from examination of the originals.

The elaborate hairstyle of the female portrait bust is based upon that of the empress Sabina, wife of Hadrian, and a date of the first half of the second century AD is likely: hairstyles fashionable in Rome could well go on for much longer in the provinces. The comparanda given are included to date them to a more limited period than is certainly assignable. These include A. Krug, *Antike Gemmen in Römisch-Germanischen Museum Köln*, Cologne, 1981, No. 201, a carnelian from the Rhineland, dated between AD 100 and 120, and No. 391, a carnelian given a date of the first quarter of the second century. Other examples are: G. M. A. Richter, *Engraved Gems of the Romans*, London, 1971, Nos 548–9, which are a carnelian in the Ashmolean Museum and a sard in the British Museum. The latter is H. B. Walters, *Catalogue of the Engraved Gems and Cameos in the British Museum*, London, 1926, No 2002 (the black agate 2001 is similar).

The worn bust appears to have been engraved on a well domed stone which is probably BC rather than AD (of course it could have been remounted much later). The head probably is female, but a couple of the comporanda are regarded as Apollo. Similar busts (none is extremely close but most are very near) are found in U. Pannuti, *Museo Archeologico Nazionale di Napoli, catalogo della collezione glittica*, Rome, 1983, No. 221, an onyx from Pompeii (hence before AD 79) and No. 223, a jacinth?, also from Pompeii, but coarse in execution; G. Platz-Horster, *Die antike Gemmen aus Xanten* i, Cologne, 1987, a burnt carnelian of the end of the first century AD; H. Guiraud, *Intailles et camées romains*, Paris, 1996, an onyx from Saint Marcel (Indre), regarded as possibly Apollo and a bit more elaborate than yours; E. Zweirlein-Diehl, *Antike Gemmen in deutschen Sammlungen* ii, *Berlin*, Munich, 1969, No. 357, a carnelian of about 90–60 BC, and regarded as Apollo.

The question which must be posed is whether the interments are those of the persons for whom the tomb was constructed. Here a combination factors may indicate that the building of the tomb had occurred much earlier. The architecture of West Tomb 1 (see below) is quite unlike that of any other tomb structure in Dakhleh or Kharga, and is largely non-Egyptian in character. In its considerable use of stone and baked brick it is only surpassed by the entirely stone-built tombs at Bashendi in Dakhleh (Mills 1983, 131; 1984, 83–5; Osing 1982). Elsewhere, elaborate architecture for tomb structures of the period occurs solely in mud brick, as, for example at Ismant el-Kharab in the North Tomb Group and South Tomb Group (Knudstad and Frey, in press), and other sites in both Dakhleh, such as at 'Beyout el-Quraysh' south of Ismant el-Kharab (Mills 1982, 98; Winlock 1936, 42), and in Kharga, at el-Bagawat (Fakhry 1951).[11] Clearly, those for whom West Tomb 1 was built were of some affluence and it might be wondered whether, despite looting, the style of burials found within it reflect a comparable level. It is instructive to compare the burials in this tomb with those dating to the late first century BCE to third century CE found in the cemetery west of the site (31/420–C5–1), which, in the better-equipped cases, had gilded- and painted-cartonnage head and foot covers (Birrell, herein) despite being interred in small, poorly-cut tombs.

The mausolea in the other groups at Ismant el-Kharab were located at a distance from the settlement, and such would probably also have been the case with the West Tombs. The enclosure in which they now stand was erected with the building of the West Church in the mid-fourth century. Prior to this the construction of Enclosures 2 and 3 would have reduced the isolation of the tombs considerably. While none of the structures within either of these enclosures has been examined, it can be reasonably inferred that they were in existence throughout the third century and possibly earlier. The major development of the Main Temple complex in Enclosure 1 can be dated to the period from Hadrian, at the very latest, to the end of the second century, with only minor additions in the early third century (Hope, in press a). The construction technique of the Doric frieze of the entablature of the façade of West Tomb 1 has details in common with that once supported by the four large baked-brick columns of the portico in front of the Main Temple. In both cases the metopes had at their centres eight-petalled wooden rosettes; in the latter instance the metopes were made of stucco attached presumably to a wooden beam. The portico of the Main Temple was probably constructed before the end of the second century CE, and possibly much earlier (Hope, in press a).

The only close parallels to West Tomb 1 are found in Libya, at Ghirza and in Wadi Nfed, where there are two stone tombs with very similar architecture (see below), both dated to the third century CE (Brogan and Smith 1984, 121–5, 208, 264–5).

To conclude, evidence to date would indicate that West Tomb 1, and probably its neighbour, was built by the mid-third century and possibly in the second century, if not earlier, and the interments discovered in it were made in the late third century or very early fourth century. What state of preservation the tomb structure was in when these burials were made is difficult to ascertain. There are no signs of repair, such as replastering, to the surviving remains; given the nature of the materials which are used in its construction, it is not unreasonable to suggest that it stood substantially intact, support for which is presented by the current remarkable state of preservation of many mud-brick mausolea of similar date in both Dakhleh and Kharga.

---

[11] The majority of these structures are imprecisely dated. None of the tombs in the North Tomb Group or South Tomb Group at Ismant el-Kharab has been examined by the Dakhleh Oasis Project and all appear to have been plundered.

The Superstructures

West Tomb 1

Description of the Remains

In situ **Remains** (Figure 1 and Plate 1)

The structure consists of a podium (width 8.835 ± 0.065 m; length 10.38 ± 0.02 m; extant height 1.33 m at south-western corner) enclosing a tomb chamber. The podium is formed by a wall of baked brick upon a rough stone foundation which retains a brick- and stone-rubble fill. A sandstone paving is laid across the top of the retaining wall and the fill. The wall (average thickness 0.76 m) preserves much of its plastered exterior surface. The podium is approached by a flight of sandstone steps (total width 3.30 m; length 2.65 m) with a balustrade (width 0.265 m) along either side. There appear to have been eight, or possibly nine, steps (depth 0.30 m, height 0.15 m).

The podium supported a central chamber (width 4.165 ± 0.005 m; length 5.205 ± 0.005 m) as indicated by the remains of the base of a stone wall (thickness 0.69 m). The outlines of corner pilasters (width 0.35 m; depth 0.05 m) survive on the north-eastern and south-western corners and there are traces of an entrance in the centre of the eastern side. Fragments from a timber door frame were found in the vicinity of the tomb. The interior of this chamber (width 2.775 ± 0.005 m; length 3.83 ± 0.01 m) contains a shaft (width 0.925 ± 0.005 m; length 0.80 m) in the south-eastern corner leading to the vaulted stone chamber below (width 2.63 ± 0.01 m; length 3.695 ± 0.015 m; height at centre 2.04 m). The chamber and shaft are constructed from ashlar blocks of sandstone.

Architectural Fragments

Two joining sections of one sandstone column shaft (surviving length 2.13 m; lower surviving diameter 0.475 ± 0.025 m, upper diameter 0.39 m) were found, apparently in their fall position, to the east of the south-eastern corner of the building (Plate 10). Fragments of white-plastered, baked-brick columns (one with upper diameter of 0.42 ± 0.02 m) were found along the south side of the building and in the cleared areas to the south-east and south-west (Plate. 11). As mentioned above, clearance of surface sand revealed fragments from three baked-brick columns on the west of the tomb. As yet it is not possible to determine the height of the columns.

The baked-brick columns indicate a peristyle at the front and along the south and west sides. Presumably it would have continued around the whole structure. The stone column is of the correct proportions to have belonged to the same order as the baked brick columns and would appear to have come from the same peristyle, probably the corner. If stone columns were also used on either side at the top of the flight of the stairs it would explain the increased thickness of the wall at these points.

A baked-brick and plaster Corinthian capital (height 0.44 m; lower diameter 0.42 ± 0.02 m) was found attached to a section of column shaft (length 0.66 m) against the south wall of the tomb with other sections from the same column (Plates 11–12). The baked-brick core of the capital, which has several sherds plastered into the top of it, had a wide acanthus leaf of plaster under each corner volute with one acanthus leaf between. The corner volutes were formed of plaster on a wooden core. In the centre of

Plate 10 West Tomb 1: Stone column and baked-brick capital south of the tomb steps.

Plate 11 West Tomb 1: Sections from baked-brick column south of the tomb.

Plate 12 West Tomb 1: detail of capital from south of the tomb, showing the emplacement for a winged Medusa head in a tondo.

the area between the corner volutes there is a wooden peg held in place by plaster, and plaster around it from some element which was once attached (Plate. 12). Near to the capital an eroded plaster head was found. Other examples from this area were set within plaster bowls and applied by means of a wooden dowel and plaster to a larger object (Figure 3c). They are of the correct size to have been positioned on the capital in place of the helices between the corner volutes. The better preserved heads enable them to be identified as winged Medusa heads. The use of Medusa heads on tombs occurs at sites such as Petra (McKenzie 1990, Plate 136b); they are also used in the Severan Forum at Leptis Magna (Lyttleton 1974, Plate 5).

Two sandstone corner volutes, with part of the abacus above and acanthus leaf below, broken off two separate Corinthian capitals were found south of the steps (Figure 4a–b). The shape of the acanthus leaf indicates that each capital tapers in sharply below the corner volutes. These fragments are similar to the volutes used upon the capitals of the baked-brick columns and so probably derive from the capitals of the stone columns used at the front of the peristyle. A pair of small sandstone animal heads, tentatively identified as lions (Figure 3a–b), were found in the same area as the stone capital fragments and possibly came from the bosses on the abaci of these capitals.

Four fragments from eight-petalled wooden rosettes (maximum diameter 0.155 ± 0.015 m) were found amongst the rubble. They are the correct size to have come from the metope of a Doric frieze of conventional proportions from the entablature above the baked brick capitals. No other indication of the order or details of the entablature were found in 1993.

The peristyle probably had four columns across the front and either four or five along the back and possibly five along the sides. As it is unlikely that the baked-brick columns could have supported the weight of a tiled roof; the tomb probably had a flat roof constructed of palm wood.

Dimensions

The building has been laid out with very precise measurements indicating that although it included more perishable building materials, such as baked brick and plaster, it was built with as much professional care as would have been taken with a more expensive, completely stone structure.

A long cubit of 0.5205 m appears to have been used for the basic design. The long cubit, or royal cubit of seven palms, in the Ptolemaic period is generally 0.523–0.525 m, but it does vary slightly. The importance is the precision of the measurements on the building itself (Figure 5): the podium has a length of 20 long cubits (10.41 m including plaster) and a width of 17 long cubits (8.85 m); the

thickness of the brick retaining wall is one and a half long cubits (including plaster 0.781 m); the central chamber is 10 long cubits in length (5.205 m) and eight long cubits wide (4.165 m). This then reveals that the width of the podium of 17 long cubits is not so surprising as it leaves three long cubits on either side of the central chamber between it and the retaining wall. The balustrade on the flight of stairs is half a long cubit wide (0.26 m).

The lowest course of the corner pilasters of the central chamber is 0.35 m wide, which is one Ptolemaic foot. The thickness of the wall of the central chamber at 0.69 m is approximately two Ptolemaic feet.

The width of the interior of the central chamber (2.78 m) is thus the exterior width of eight long cubits minus the wall thickness. This dimension is also used for the width of the staircase to which the balustrade of half a cubit is added on either side to give a total width of the flight of stairs of 3.30 m. When these steps are centrally placed it then leaves 2.735 m on either side. The length of the flight of steps (2.65 m) is approximately five long cubits (2.63 m). The height of the baked-brick capital 0.44 m is one short cubit of six palms.

West Tomb 2

Sometime after the construction of West Tomb 1, West Tomb 2 was erected against it, with its own platform, having a retaining wall only on its east, north and west sides. It is less well preserved than Tomb 1, but comprises a podium approached by a flight of sandstone steps; there was a central chamber with a vaulted burial chamber below also constructed of sandstone. It would thus appear to have been perhaps of a similar design to Tomb 1. Work on Tomb 2 was restricted to surface clearance and the excavation of the burial chamber. Until the area surrounding it has been excavated it is not possible to detail its architecture further.

Flat-Roofed Peripteral Structures

To summarize from the present evidence as indicated, West Tomb 1 appears to have had a podium, approached by a narrow flight of approximately eight steps, supporting a peristyle with Corinthian capitals, probably with four columns across the front and five along the sides. It perhaps had a Doric frieze on the entablature and probably had a flat roof. There is a vaulted tomb below the central chamber, reached by a shaft in the corner of the room.

West Tomb 1, and possibly the adjoining Tomb 2, are the only examples surviving in Egypt of structures of this design. However, a stone structure of very similar design survives at Wadi Ghirza in Libya (North Tomb A: Brogan and Smith 1984, 121–25).[12] This has in common the

---

[12] In the search for parallels to West Tomb 1 the assistance of Professor F. Sear, University of Melbourne, is gratefully acknowledged.

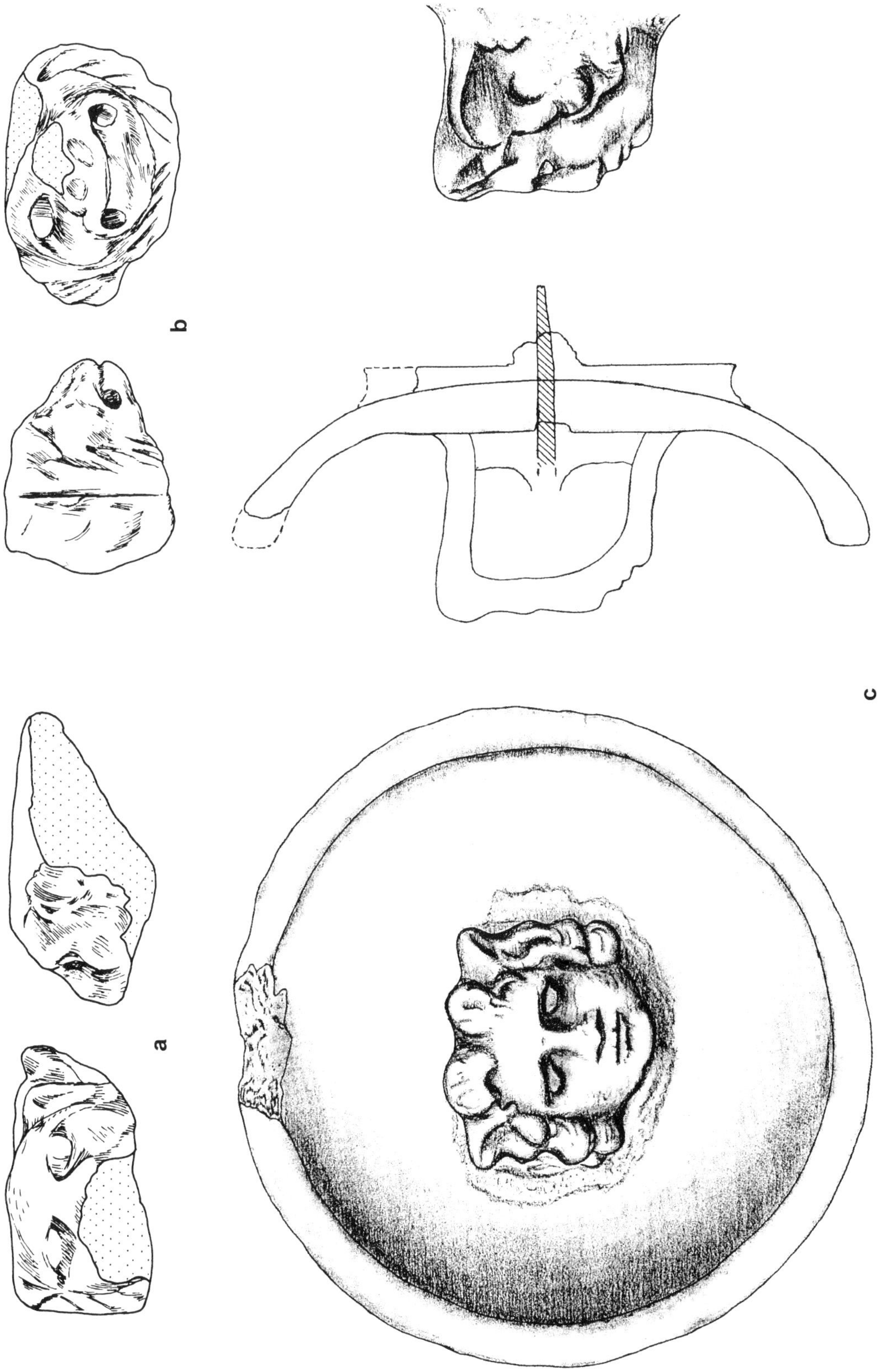

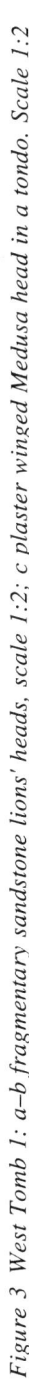

Figure 3 *West Tomb 1: a–b fragmentary sandstone lions' heads, scale 1:2; c plaster winged Medusa head in a tondo. Scale 1:2*

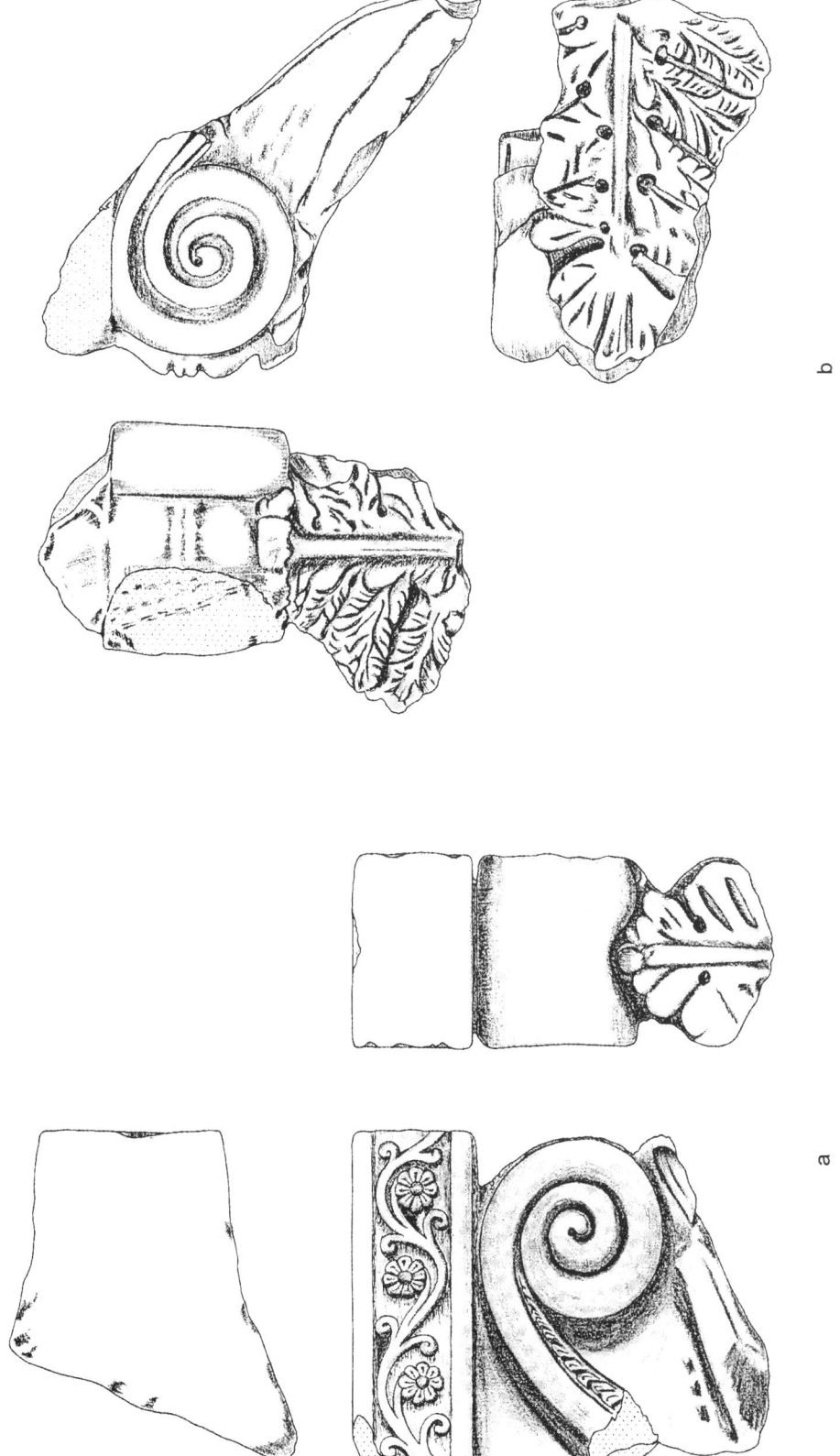

Figure 4 West Tomb 1: Fragments of two sandstone capitals found south of the steps. Scale 1:3.

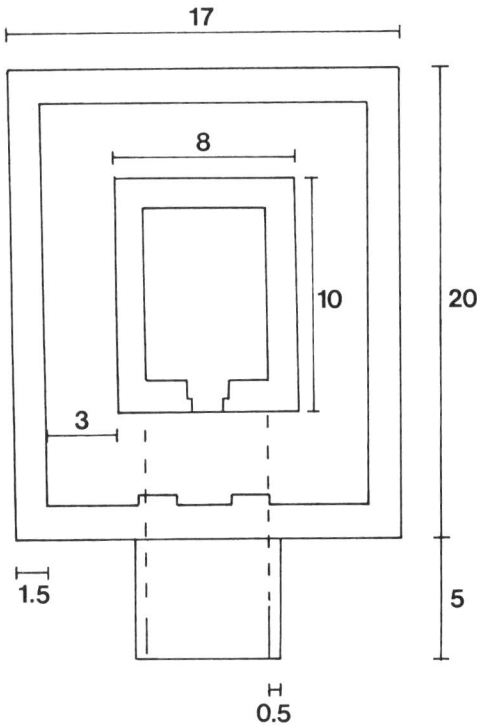

Figure 5 West Tomb 1 showing dimensions in long cubits.

Figure 6 Sketch (after Price and Trell, Figure 508) of a coin of Juba I (60–46 BCE) of Mauretania, showing flat-roofed, peristyle strucure on a podium approached by a flight of steps.

podium and flight of steps, a tomb below the central chamber and a peristyle of columns supporting an entablature with a Doric frieze. It also had four columns across the front and five along the sides. Notably, although constructed of stone, the Libyan example has a flat roof. The entablature has survived to its full height around all of this structure with a sima along the top at both the front and back, not only along the sides. Thus, it did not have a pediment. It has been dated to the third century CE. (Brogan and Smith 1984, 125, 212) as has another similar tomb in Wadi Nfed (Brogan and Smith 1984, 264–5).

The example from Ismant el-Kharab is of particular interest because not only are related structures depicted on North African coins from the first century CE (e.g. Figure 6) but also on Roman coins from Alexandria, an example of one of which has been found at the site (Plate 13). The Alexandrian examples are clearly of a major monument in the city which has never been satisfactorily identified. Poole (1892, xciii) interpreted it as one structure: a large altar which he suggested was part of the Kaisareion. More recent interpretations have been based upon two assumptions. First, that the image on the coins consists of more than one structure combined into the one image on the plane of the coin. Second, that when a

Plate 13 Bronze drachma of Antoninus Pius (138–161 CE) from House 3 showing flat-roofed, peristyle structure on a podium; diameter 32 mm.

peristyle structure with a classical entablature, but no pediment, is depicted it is either a peristyle court or a gate, but not a temple. Thus, Handler (1971, 69) suggests the Alexandrian coins depict an altar in a temenos with the flames depicted above the entablature of the temple enclosure. Price and Trell (1977, 21) interpret it as "a combination of gate and altar" "in which the flaming altar appears to form the top part of a columned portico. In fact, the figure of Tyche stands between the columns to identify the cult of the sanctuary, and the architrave of the 'gate' forms the top of a Near Eastern 'horned' altar".

However, West Tomb 1 at Ismant el-Kharab indicates the existence in Graeco-Roman Egypt of an architectural type consisting of a peristyle structure with a classical entablature, a flat roof and no pediment. It was supported by a podium and contained a chamber, which in a temple would have been the cella. This is precisely the basic building type depicted on the Alexandrian coins, which in addition would have had a statue in the cella and the roof used for the fire altar. The surviving Alexandrian coins all depict a fire on top of the structure. Fire altars are known in Egypt from the Ptolemaic Period (Quaegebeur 1993)[13] and the use of temple roofs for various rituals and ceremonies is well known.

Conclusion

As a classical architectural form the idea of a peristyle structure on a podium with a cella and a flat roof and no pediment would not have appeared surprising as a result of local Egyptian or Near Eastern influence where flat roofs were so common. The absence of a pediment would have been no more noticeable than it is to the modern eye on the Lincoln Centre or the Lincoln Memorial or the National Library in Canberra where the allusion to classical architecture is achieved by the peristyle itself around the building.

Thus, West Tomb 1 would appear to be the only definite example surviving in Egypt of an otherwise 'lost' building type which was the form used for a major monument in Alexandria. Until the discovery of this tomb at Ismant el-Kharab it had not been possible to suggest that these coin depictions are a fairly accurate reflection of an Alexandrian building rather than a schematized drawing.

The precise laying out of West Tomb 1 indicates that high quality buildings were made of more transitory materials than stone. This suggests that far more good quality classical architecture has probably been lost in Egypt than has previously been indicated by the surviving remains of stone architecture (see Bailey 1990).

---

[13] A graffito of two horned altars with a seated figure and another of a single altar are to be found incised into the pavement south of the central chamber of West Tomb 1.

Epigraphy at Ismant el-Kharab 1992–94: Interim Observations

Olaf E. Kaper

During the 1992–94 field seasons the epigraphic work at Ismant el-Kharab was mainly focussed upon the study of the painted-plaster decoration of Shrine I. This shrine has been introduced already in previous reports (Bowen et al. 1993, 19–20; Hope 1991, 48–9; Hope et al. 1989, 8–12, 15–16; 1992, 45–7; Kaper 1991, 64–6), so I will outline only its main features here. A plan of the shrine isolated from its surroundings is shown in Figure 1. It was built in mud brick and entirely plastered and painted. Excavation has concentrated on the inner room of the shrine, which measures approximately 4.8 by 12.0 m and which is preserved to a height of 3.5 m in the south-western corner above the original floor level. Its original height is estimated at 5.0 m. The room is filled with the remains of its vaulted ceiling which collapsed in antiquity onto a layer of wind-blown sand.

The excavations within the shrine are proceeding now at a quicker pace than in the initial years after its discovery. The methods of lifting the painted plaster fragments from the collapse, as well as the techniques involved in their subsequent treatment, have improved much, largely as a result of the efforts of the chief conservator at Ismant el-Kharab, Michelle Berry of the Museum of Victoria.

During the excavations the plaster fragments are stored on numbered trays which relate to their exact find spot. A lengthy process then involves the cleaning and sorting of fragments, initial consolidation of the plaster if necessary and reconstruction. After a group of fragments has been reassembled the conservator provides the finished assemblage with a backing, so that the result can be drawn, photographed and stored. The drawings of the reconstructed sections will then be combined with those of the larger segments of plaster which still adhere to the vaulting bricks or to the walls of the shrine. This process proved to be successful when, during the 1994 season, a first series of paintings could be completely reconstructed on paper (now published in Kaper 1997).

Figure 2 contains an example of a scene which is still in the process of reconstruction. The line drawing shows Hathor of Dendera presenting a necklace in a scene which was painted on the northern half of the vault within the uppermost register. In this case, the plaster has been preserved largely intact upon four separate brick segments which have been reassembled in the drawing. The missing elements between the bricks will be drawn in later because here the thin layer of painted plaster has shattered into

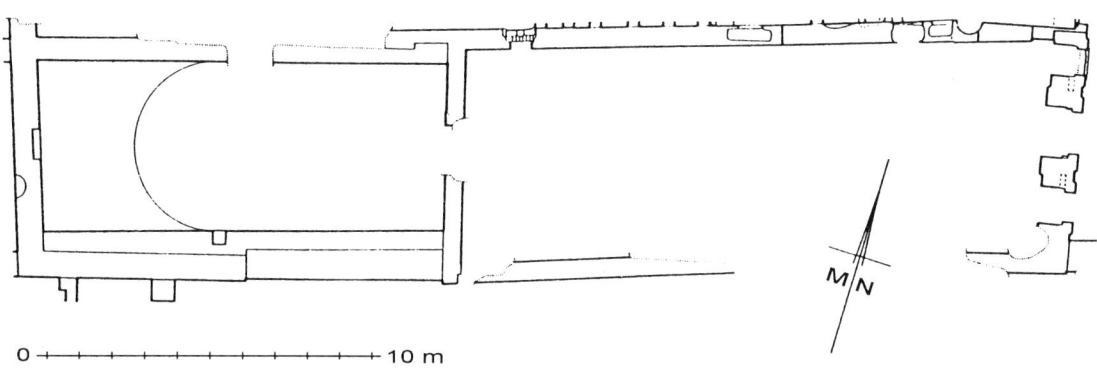

Figure 1 Plan of Shrine I (after a plan by James E. Knudstad).

Figure 2

numerous small fragments which will necessitate much study before they can be reassembled in their original context. From the study of the loose fragments from this scene we already know that the table at the feet of Hathor of Dendera supported another necklace.

It is a fortunate coincidence that the Franco-Egyptian Centre for the Study of the Temples of Karnak (CFETK) has also recently em-barked on a very similar project in connection with the excavation of a large mortuary structure connected with the cult of Osiris (Coulon et al. 1997).[1]

This building received painted decoration in the reign of Ptolemy IV Philopator upon a thick layer of plaster. During mutual visits, the experiences with various methods of treating the painted-plaster fragments at each site have been compared. At Karnak, the material differs from Ismant el-Kharab in style and subject matter and also in the thicker layer of plaster used. However, the technical aspects of its conservation and restoration are largely similar and a continued exchange of information should be beneficial for both teams.

The Decorative Scheme of Shrine I

The schematic drawing reproduced in Figure 3 indicates our current understanding of the shrine's overall decorative scheme. The rear wall has as its focus a niche with a plaster shell motif, which probably once contained a cult image. The dado of the room on the rear and side walls is approximately 2.0 m in height and was painted in classical style. The rear wall above this dado was decorated with pharaonic-style paintings (Plate 1). The side walls below the springing of the vault contained one register with pharaonic-style paintings, measuring on average 55.0 cm in height. The vault itself was largely painted in the pharaonic style, divided into three registers on either side, which measure each 76.0 cm (1.5 Egyptian cubits) in height. The central band of the vault, which I estimate at approximately 1.5 m in width, again contained classical-style paintings. The border between the two styles was marked by a large-scale hieroglyphic inscription across the entire length of the room. In Figure 3, the location of the pharaonic style paintings has been indicated.

Thus far, the excavations have only exposed the western end of the room and part of the northern wall. A door was set within this wall, the jambs of which were also decorated with pharaonic paintings. The cornice above this door contained both classical and pharaonic elements. From the evidence of small probes, the decoration in the eastern half of the room seems to conform to a similar pattern throughout.

Upon the northern wall a total of eighteen graffiti in ink and charcoal has been recorded. These show boats and other figurative elements; others are copies of decorative patterns upon the ceiling of the shrine itself. Only one text appears upon this wall, written in Sahidic Coptic, recording the use of the shrine by two gooseherds and their flock one night in the month Paoni of an unnamed year. From such reuse of the shrine possibly date the mutilations of the figures upon the walls and the vault. All faces within the lower registers have been attacked, as well as some figurative elements within the classical-style paintings of the dado.

---

[1] I thank Sylvie Marchand and Laurent Coulon of the Franco-Egyptian Centre at Karnak for showing this material to me.

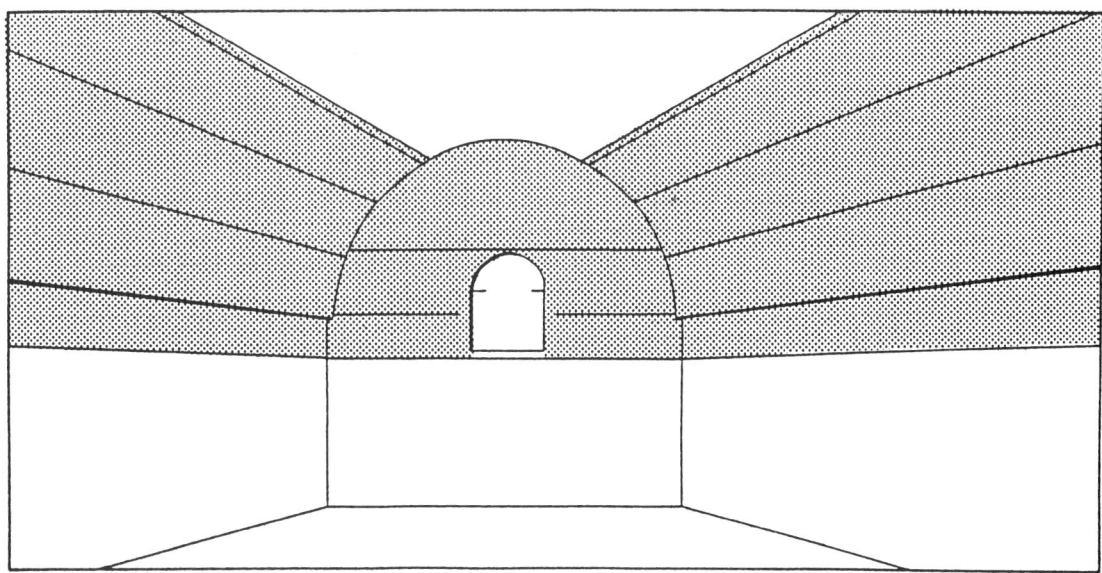

Figure 3 Decorative scheme of Shrine I; shaded areas indicate the location of pharaonic decoration.

Plate 1 Rear wall of Shrine I.

Contents of the Paintings

The study of the pharaonic paintings can only be undertaken properly after the reconstruction of a series of individual scenes has been completed. Many of the scenes, the interpretation of which at this moment present problems, will eventually become easier to understand as their reconstruction progresses. Currently one of the main general concerns is the date of the paintings. Unusually, Shrine I does not depict an emperor-pharaoh in the offering scenes. Instead, the registers contain several series of gods in interaction, or they depict priests carrying offerings to the gods. Our current working hypothesis sets the date of construction and decoration of the shrine together with that of the principal building phase of the Main Temple in the late first to early second century CE (Hope, in press a).

Shrine I was dedicated to the gods Tutu (Tithoes) and Neith together. The decoration in the southern half of the room emphasizes figures of Tutu, while the northern half emphasizes Neith (Hope et al. 1989, 16). This division of the subject matter over the walls of the sanctuary has not been imposed too strictly, because Tutu and Neith are also depicted together in several scenes of a more general nature.

Shrine I presents us with the opportunity to become acquainted with the ancient methods of decorating a vault divided into several registers. Other vaulted shrines are known from ancient Egypt,[2] but no other example has been found with several registers upon the vault. One observation which can already be made about Shrine I concerns the general conventions of representing the deities within the different registers. As a rule upon temple walls, the deities are represented in a standing posture within the *soubassement* and in the first register, and seated in all registers above. A variant scheme governs the decoration of doorways, in which all gods upon the jambs are represented standing and only upon the lintel are they shown seated. The decoration of Shrine I now adds a third variety, which is not unlike the latter. Upon the vault of Shrine I all deities are represented standing, as on the jambs of a gate, except in the uppermost register, where the final deity at the rear end of the shrine is represented seated upon a throne. A complicating element here is the decoration of the shrine's walls below the springing of the vault, where the deities at the rear end of the room are again shown seated. Whether these rules were ever standardized will only be known when another example of this type of building is found.

The style of the pharaonic paintings in Shrine I, as far as can be judged at this early stage, is both free and elaborate, without becoming unconventional. The painting

Plate 2 Vaulting block from Shrine I preserving representations of two of the Seven Hathors.

of Hathor rendered in Figure 2 and those in Plate 2 show the great attention paid to details in the goddess' dress and crown which are all according to conventional design. When compared to reliefs in contemporary temples elsewhere, such as at Dendera, parallels for the individual details in the paintings can often be found,[3] but on the whole the Kellis paintings combine a larger number of individual details in one scene. The shrine's painters displayed great freedom and also ability in combining different elements in rendering the figures on the walls. The minor deities especially have often been provided with additional elements, such as offering stands (Figure 2 and Plate 2) or appropriate hieroglyphic symbols represented at their feet. In my opinion, it is only this trait which allows a distinction to be made between the iconography of painted versus sculpted temple decoration. In all other respects a temple relief is simply a more

---

[2] e.g., the Hathor shrine of Tuthmose III at Deir el-Bahari, cf., G. Pinch, *Votive Offerings to Hathor*, Oxford, 1993, 9–12 with references. The use of decorated vaults is more commonly attested in tombs, e.g., at Deir el-Medineh, cf., B. Bruyère, *La tombe no. 1 de Sen-nedjem à Deir el-Médineh*, Cairo, 1959.

[3] Some parallels for the crown of Hathor in Figure 2 are listed in J. Vandier, 'Iousâas et (Hathor)-Nebet-hétépet, *Revue de Égyptologie* 17 (1965), 137 (3b).

permanent version of a painted scene (cf. Schäfer 1986, chapter 3). Relief scenes were, of course, meant to be finished in paint, which would add all the details not rendered by the sculptor (see, for example, the photograph in Cauville 1990, 8).

A detailed outline of the decoration of Shrine I will be presented elsewhere. A small number of scenes have now been identified, showing a wide variety of themes with complex and original details, but all of these will need further reconstruction and study before an assessment of their significance can be made. Another matter which will remain unresolved for now, is the function of Shrine I within the temple complex as a whole.

The Temple Complex and its Gods

The temple complex at Kellis consists of five different enclosures (Figure 4), of which only a fraction has yet been touched by excavations. From the walls visible upon the surface of the site the layout of the internal structures can be partly determined without excavation. The location of the main structures within the complex can be established in relation to the axis of Enclosure 1, the largest of the five enclosures. In this way, the position of the Main Temple and of the adjacent Shrine I was established during

a survey of the site in 1981 (Mills 1982, 99). The function of Enclosures 2–4 may not be religious in nature. Perhaps we should compare them to the enclosure adjacent to the temple at Dush in Kharga, which may have functioned as a defendable storehouse (Reddé 1990, 288). The recent excavations within Enclosure 4 have shown how unexpected the contents of these enclosures can be. Elsewhere in this volume, Hope and McKenzie describe two early stone tombs which were found within this enclosure beside a fourth-century church (Bowen et al. 1993, 21–25).

We may safely assume that the temple complex contained three main separate shrines. The most important of these was the Main Temple. Second in importance was the West Temple, which, like the Main Temple, was built of stone and its reliefs plastered and painted. These two buildings qualify as major structures within their predominantly mud-brick surroundings. The mud-brick Shrine I should be added to these, simply because of its size and its more elaborate painted decoration. Apart from Shrine I, three other structures around the Main Temple can plausibly be identified as shrines by their location or ground plan; however, none compares to Shrine I in size or decoration.

From the decoration of the three major buildings, the principal gods of the temple complex can be identified as the gods Tutu, Neith and Tapsais. The distinctive locations

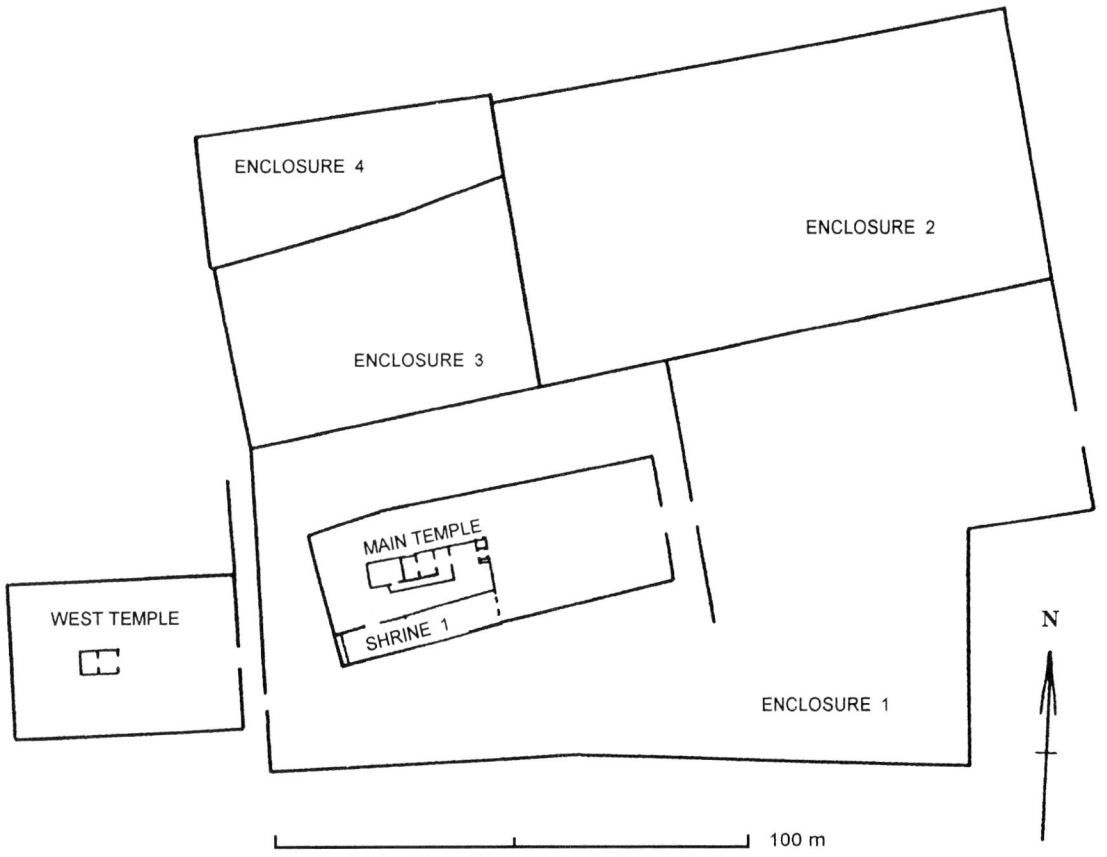

Figure 4 Schematic plan of the temple complex at Kellis (based upon a drawing by J. E. Knudstad).

where the main gods are found upon the temple walls are: (1) the rear wall of the sanctuary, as preserved in Shrine I, (2) the lower registers of doorways, as preserved in the West Temple, and (3) the lintels of doorways, as preserved in the Main Temple. It appears from the reliefs and inscriptions on the doorway into the West Temple that this sanctuary was built specifically for the cult of Neith and Tapsais.

The gods of ancient Kellis are remarkable in themselves. Tutu was one of the last gods to be added to the Egyptian pantheon. His increased popularity is apparent throughout Egypt during the Ptolemaic and Roman periods. At this time, however, new major temples were only rarely founded and we find that the god was usually incorporated into already existing cults.[4] The Kellis temple is the first location known in which Tutu became the major deity. The goddess Neith, on the other hand, was venerated in several major temples (el-Sayed 1982). She is one of the oldest deities known from Egypt, being attested already three thousand years before the construction of the Kellis temple. Her role in relation to Tutu is that of the god's mother. Finally, the goddess Tapsais is of an even more recent origin than Tutu, because her name is not known from any other source in Egypt (Kaper and Worp 1995). We can, therefore, conclude that the addition of Tapsais to Tutu and Neith took place only in Kellis, probably as late as the Roman Period when the Kellis temple was built.

By adding the West Temple to the complex, the relationship between Neith and Tapsais was provided with special recognition in a separate cult. In accordance with the revised cultic layout of the temple complex, Neith would at this stage have 'moved out' into the new West Temple. Her position in Shrine I remained unaltered, since no changes were made to its decoration. It is important, therefore, to establish, whether at this stage any changes were made to the cults in the Main Temple.

The Main Temple was above all dedicated to Tutu, as was already apparent from the dedicatory inscription found on the site by A. Fakhry in 1969 (Wagner 1973, 177–80). This inscription has been dated to the reign of Antoninus Pius. However, I think that the Main Temple accorded a special position to Tapsais. This conclusion can be drawn from one of the Greek papyri found within the temple, which dates from 298–300 CE. It mentions a priest named Aurelius Stonios who was the priest 'of Tithoes and Tnephersais'. The name Tnephersais also occurs in Shrine I as a variant of Tapsais (Kaper and Worp 1995). Stonios' title seems to imply a dual dedication of the Main Temple.

Unfortunately we cannot be certain about this, but it receives some confirmation from the text upon a bronze votive statuette found in the contra-temple of the Main Temple (Kaper and Worp 1995) which mentions the same combination of Tutu and Tapsais. No information is forthcoming concerning this from the remains of the Main Temple and its reliefs, due to their extremely fragmentary preservation. The reconstructed lintels of the entrance gateways of the temple emphasize only Tutu, as does the dedicatory inscription of Antoninus Pius, while Neith and Tapsais appear in secondary positions (for Neith and Tutu see Hope et al. 1989, 14 , Figure 5). The only other relief which allows identification of its subject matter depicts Tapsais. This relief dates to the reign of Pertinax (193 CE) and originates from a door jamb within the contra-temple (Bowen et al. 1993, 18–9; Kaper and Worp 1995). It is tempting to interpret these combined data to indicate a preference for Tapsais over Neith within the Main Temple. Unfortunately, the material is too scarce to elevate this idea above the level of a hypothesis.

Conclusions

The temple complex at Ismant el-Kharab was dedicated to the three deities Tutu, Neith and Tapsais, but their cults were spread at a certain stage over three different shrines within the complex. Shrine I was dedicated to Tutu and Neith, and the West Temple to Tapsais and Neith, while the Main Temple became, according to the hypothesis outlined above, dedicated in particular to Tutu and Tapsais. The three shrines thus each emphasized the relationship between two of the three main deities. The cultic detachment of the local triad would have corresponded with specific ritual activities within the three shrines and mutually between the individual shrines. This, however, remains a subject for speculation, partly because of the unique character of the Kellis temples. A similar cultic trisection within one temple complex does not seem to occur elsewhere in Egypt.

Further study of the epigraphic material in the coming years will, it is hoped, provide further confirmation of this hypothesis. Above all, the dedication of the Main Temple should be solved for the different periods of its use. The role of the different sanctuaries within the complex as a whole will be another urgent matter to be defined. What has already become clear is that the Kellis temples in all of their complexity display the full vitality of Egyptian religion and thought throughout the second century.

---

[4] On Tutu see J. Quaegebeur, 'Tithoes', *Lexikon der Ägyptologie* VI, Wiesbaden, 1986, columns 602–6 with references. A monograph on Tutu is being prepared by the present author.

Glass from the 1993 Excavations at Ismant el-Kharab

Carla Marchini

The Cache from House 4

During the 1994 season I began a study of the glass from the excavations at Ismant el-Kharab. This article comprises mainly a catalogue of the glass found in House 4.[1] This house lies due east of the entrance into Enclosure 1 which contains the Main Temple of Tutu, in the residential quarter of Area A. It has not yet been completely cleared, but it seems to be composed of a central core of rooms, with additions on the east, south and west. House 4 provided a large quantity of material, including basketry, coins, faience objects, household crafts, inscribed wooden boards, ostraka, papyri and pottery, and the largest single deposit of glass found at the site to date. Other parts of the site have yielded a variety of fragments from different shapes of vessels, some of which is also discussed here.

Dating

The dating of House 4 has been established within the fourth century CE thanks to the pottery and coins found during the excavations (Bowen et al. 1993, 26–7). In general the glass seems to be of the same date, and we should note the occurrence of fragments from two conical lamps, a form only used from the fourth century onwards (Auth 1991, 1143). Some of the pieces are not contemporary. This is not surprising as glass could be kept for many years (see below).

Terminology

The terminology employed herein follows that of Harden's (1936) study of material from Karanis and Hayes' (1975) publication of the glass in the Royal Ontario Museum. These still seem to be the best sources for the study of Roman glass found in Egypt.

Objects

The pieces belonging to this group were found associated with a woven fibre basket almost at surface level, deposit 1a, in Room N. This room forms part of a complex on the north side of the central core of rooms of the house which were not excavated other than for the removal of some surface sand to delineate the extent of House 4. It is uncertain whether they are an integral part of the house or whether they represent an adjacent, separate structure. It may be assumed that this northern group of rooms is preserved, like the rooms which are definitely part of House 4, to first floor level. We do not know whether the glass vessels were placed in the basket to be protected or stored because of their extreme fragility, but either is possible. As we see at Karanis (Harden 1936, 34), glass could be stored in baskets, large pots or wooden boxes, sometimes together with valued ceramics, such as terra sigillate (et similia). From this particular feature of the find we can deduce that the group probably had a special use or importance. The pieces are not all contemporary, but as was noted previously, in a country like Egypt precious objects might be preserved for generations and glass was certainly considered a valued commodity at least until the fourth century (Harden 1936, 25 n. 4). This does, of course, create problems for the dating and interpretation of the objects. It is not possible, as yet, to determine whether glass was produced locally or imported.

Range of Shapes

The forms belonging to this group are: deep, shallow bowls with base ring and decorated with incised criss-cross designs, a form widely distributed throughout Egypt, conical lamps which either stood in a tripod or were suspended from the ceiling (Auth 1991, 1143, 1145),

---

[1] A brief description and plan of House 4 are contained in Bowen et al. 1993, 25–7.

jugs and flasks with handles and spouts, beakers and drinking cups.

Colour

The most usual colour within this group is green, in varying shades, a colour easily obtained from the copper and iron impurities contained in the sand used in its manufacture (Harden 1936, 6). Other colours are brown (Harden 1936, 7), turquoise (Lucas 1962, 188), yellow and purple (Lucas 1962, 187), which in Dakhleh seems to occur more frequently than at other parts of Egypt. Three of the pieces are made of transparent glass.

Techniques and Decoration

All of the glass is blown; decoration was executed with metal or wooden tools after firing. A criss-cross design on the base rings of deep bowls is widely used; this is a distinctive feature of Egyptian bowls of this period (Auth 1991, 1143). Other decoration comprises pinched body ribs and cut lines on the rims. There are fine examples of ribbed handles on flasks and jugs, and also spouts of different colours contrasting with the body colour.

Fabric

The fabric typology which has been adopted is that of Hayes (1975, 132), but it may need modification in the light of chemical analyses which are to be conducted upon various samples.

Fabric 1: very fine, colourless or transparent, though sometimes pale green is visible in the breaks; used for luxury objects (Harden's fabrics 1 and 2).

Fabric 2: thick and bubbly, deep green; a cheap material used for commercial purposes – bottle ware (Harden's fabric 8).

Fabric 3: green and bubbly; cheap glass which is a transitional type from Roman to Coptic glass (Harden's fabric 8).

Fabric 4: thin, transparent or coloured glass, often bubbly, of inferior quality with impurities and a wide range of colours including blue and purple; Coptic table ware (Harden's fabrics 3–7).

Fabric 5: very fine, thin-walled glass of excellent quality used for toilet flasks; can be confused with Islamic glass.

The Catalogue

The individual pieces are referred to by their object inventory number from which the site prefix, 31/420–D6–1, has been omitted.

The following abbreviations are used:

Rd = rim diameter; Ht = height; Bd = base diameter; Nd = neck diameter.

Harden: reference to Harden's (1936) classification of the Karanis material.

1. A/6/293   Figure 1a
Base ring from a deep bowl, decorated with oblique lines.
Colour: green   Dimensions: Bd = 5 cm
Fabric: 4   Harden: III A I (b) 2 Date: IV

2. A/6/294   Figure 1b
Rim from deep bowl, folded outward.
Colour: green   Dimensions: Rd = 16 cm
Fabric: 4   Harden: III A I (a)   Date: IV

3. A/6/295   Figure 1c
Rim and neck from a tall-necked flask with double folded rim.
Colour: transparent   Dimensions: Rd = 4.8 cm
Fabric: 1   Harden: IX   Date: late II – early IV

4. A/6/296   Figure 1d
Fragments from the rim and body of a conical lamp, probably with a solid pointed base; unworked rim and vertical fluting on body.
Colour: pale green   Dimensions: Rd = 9 cm
Fabric: 4   Harden: VI A I   Date: IV

5. A/6/297   Figure 1e
Fragments from the rim of a shallow bowl, probably on a base ring; inward-folded rim.
Colour: mixed green and purple   Dimensions: Rd = 20 cm
Fabric: 4   Harden: II A 2   Date: IV

6. A/6/298   Figure 1f
Fragmentary deep bowl with base ring and rounded rim.
Colour: pale green   Dimensions: Rd = 15 cm; Bd = 7.1 cm; Ht = 8.8 cm
Fabric: 4   Harden: III A III (a) Date: IV

7. A/6/299   Figure 1g
Rim and neck from a tall-necked flask with outward-folded rim.
Colour: pale turquoiseDimensions: Rd = 3.8 cm
Fabric: 4   Harden: IX   Date: late III – early IV

8. A/6/300   Figure 1h
Fragments from the rim of a shallow bowl with coil rim.
Colour: green   Dimensions: Rd = 14 cm
Fabric: 4   Harden: II A IV (a) Date: IV

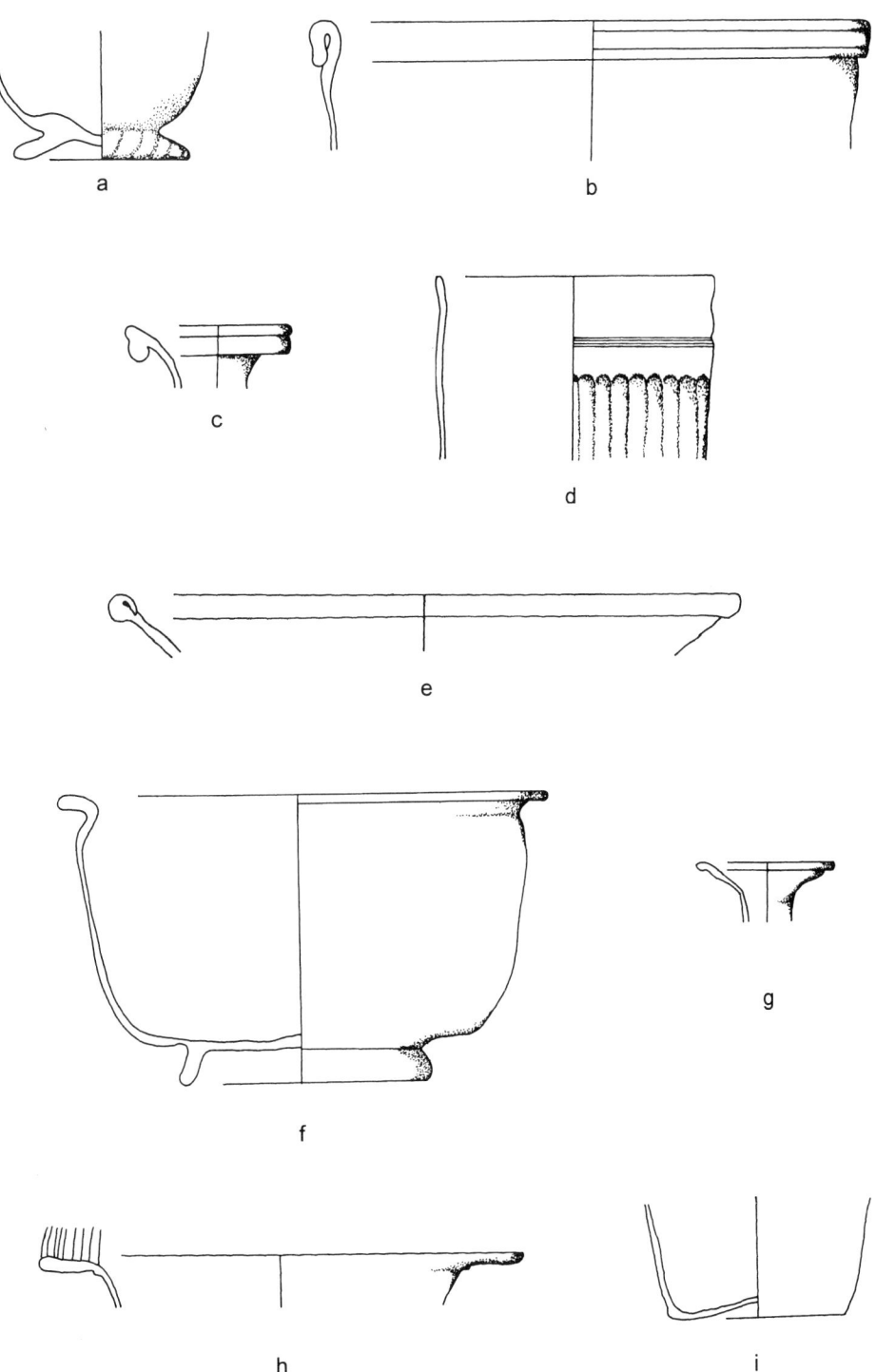

Figure 1 Glass from House 4, Room N cache. Scale 1:2

9. A/6/301 Figure 1i
Fragments from the base and body of a beaker with very thin walls.
Colour: transparent Dimensions: Bd = 5 cm
Fabric: 1 Harden: V A Date: IV

10. A/6/302 Figure 2a
Fragments from the rim of a shallow bowl with coil rim.
Colour: pale green Dimensions: Rd = 14 cm
Fabric: 4 Harden: II A IV (a) Date: IV

11. A/6/303 Figure 2b
Fragments from the rim of a deep bowl with outward-folded rim.
Colour: green Dimensions: Rd =10 cm
Fabric: 4 Harden: III A I Date: IV

12. A/6/304 Figure 2c
Fragments from the rim of a shallow bowl with inward-folded rim.
Colour: pale green Dimensions: Rd = 9 cm
Fabric: 4 Harden: II A II Date: IV

13. A/6/305 Figure 2d
Fragments from the rim of a shallow bowl with inward-folded rim.
Colour: pale green Dimensions: Rd = 14 cm
Fabric: 4 Harden: II A II Date: IV

14. A/6/306 Figure 2e
Fragments from the rim of a deep bowl with rounded rim.
Colour: deep purple Dimensions: Rd =14 cm
Fabric: 4 Harden: III A III Date: IV

15. A/6/307 Figure 2f
Fragments from the rim and body of a deep bowl with polished rim.
Colour: deep purple Dimensions: Rd = 9.6 cm
Fabric: 4 Harden: III A V Date: IV

16. A/6/308 Figure 2g
Fragmentary handled jug with concave neck and base coil; the handle and base coil are made of different coloured glass.
Colour: body is purple, handle and base coil are pale green
Dimensions: Rd = 3 cm; Bd = 2.6 cm; Ht = estimated, 9 cm
Fabric: 4 Harden: XI A II (a) Date: late III – early IV

17. A/6/309 Figure 2h
Fragments from the rim of a deep bowl with double, outward-folded rim (? footed bowl).
Colour: purple Dimensions: Rd = 14 cm
Fabric: 4 Harden: III A I Date: IV

18. A/6/310 Figure 2i
Fragments from the rim of a deep bowl with inward-folded rim (? footed bowl).
Colour: purple Dimensions: Rd = 11 cm
Fabric: 4 Harden: III A II Date: IV

19. A/6/311 Figure 2j
Fragments from the rim of a cup with s-shaped profile and thin walls.

Colour: transparent Dimensions: Rd = 9.5 cm
Fabric: 1 Harden: VII A I (a) Date: IV

20. A/6/312 Figure 3a
Fragmentary deep bowl with base ring and double-folded rim. The base ring is plain.
Colour: pale green Dimensions: Rd = 10.5 cm; Bd = 5 cm; Ht = restored, 6.5 cm
Fabric: 4 Harden: III A IV (a) Date: IV

21. A/6/313 Figure 3b
Fragmentary deep bowl with base ring and coil rim. The base ring has criss-cross design.
Colour: transparent with purple undulations in the base ring.
Dimensions: Rd = 8.2 cm; Bd = 4.2 cm; Ht = 5.4 cm.
Fabric: 1 Harden: III A IV (a) Date: IV

22. A/6/314 Figure 3c
Fragments from the rim of a deep bowl with outward-folded rim.
Colour: brown Dimensions: Rd = 9.2 cm
Fabric: 4 Harden: III A I Date: IV

23. A/6/315 Figure 3d
Fragments from the plain base ring of a deep bowl.
Colour: pale green Dimensions: Bd = 5.6 cm
Fabric: 4 Harden: III A Date: IV

24. A/6/316 Figure 3e
Fragmentary deep bowl with base ring and rounded rim. The base ring has criss-cross design.
Colour: pale purple Dimensions: Rd = 8 cm; Bd = 4.4 cm; Ht = restored, 6 cm
Fabric: 4 Harden: III A III (b) Date: IV

25. A/6/317 Figure 3f
Fragmentary tall-necked, one-handled flask with spout, and a coiled rim; bichrome.
Colour: body is pale green; rim, handle and spout are green with red veining.
Dimensions: Rd = 3.5 cm; Nd = 1.4 cm
Fabric: 1 Harden: IX B Date: late III – early IV

26. A/6/318 Figure 3g
Fragmentary deep stemmed bowl, with a double outward-folded rim and base ring, which has criss-cross design.
Colour: pale purple Dimensions: Rd = 8.4 cm; Bd = 4 cm; Ht = 2.6 cm
Fabric: 4 Harden: IV B I (b) Date: IV

27. A/6/319 Figure 3h
Fragments from a from a conical lamp with hollow base.
Colour: body is pale green and base is dark green
Dimensions: Bd = 2.4 cm; Ht = 6.3 cm
Fabric: 4 Harden: VI B Date: IV

28. A/6/320 Figure 3i
Fragments from the base and body of a deep bowl with indented base, very thin walls and pinched-rib decoration on body.
Colour: pale green Dimensions: Bd = 3.2 cm; Ht = 2.3 cm
Fabric: 1 Harden: III B Date: IV

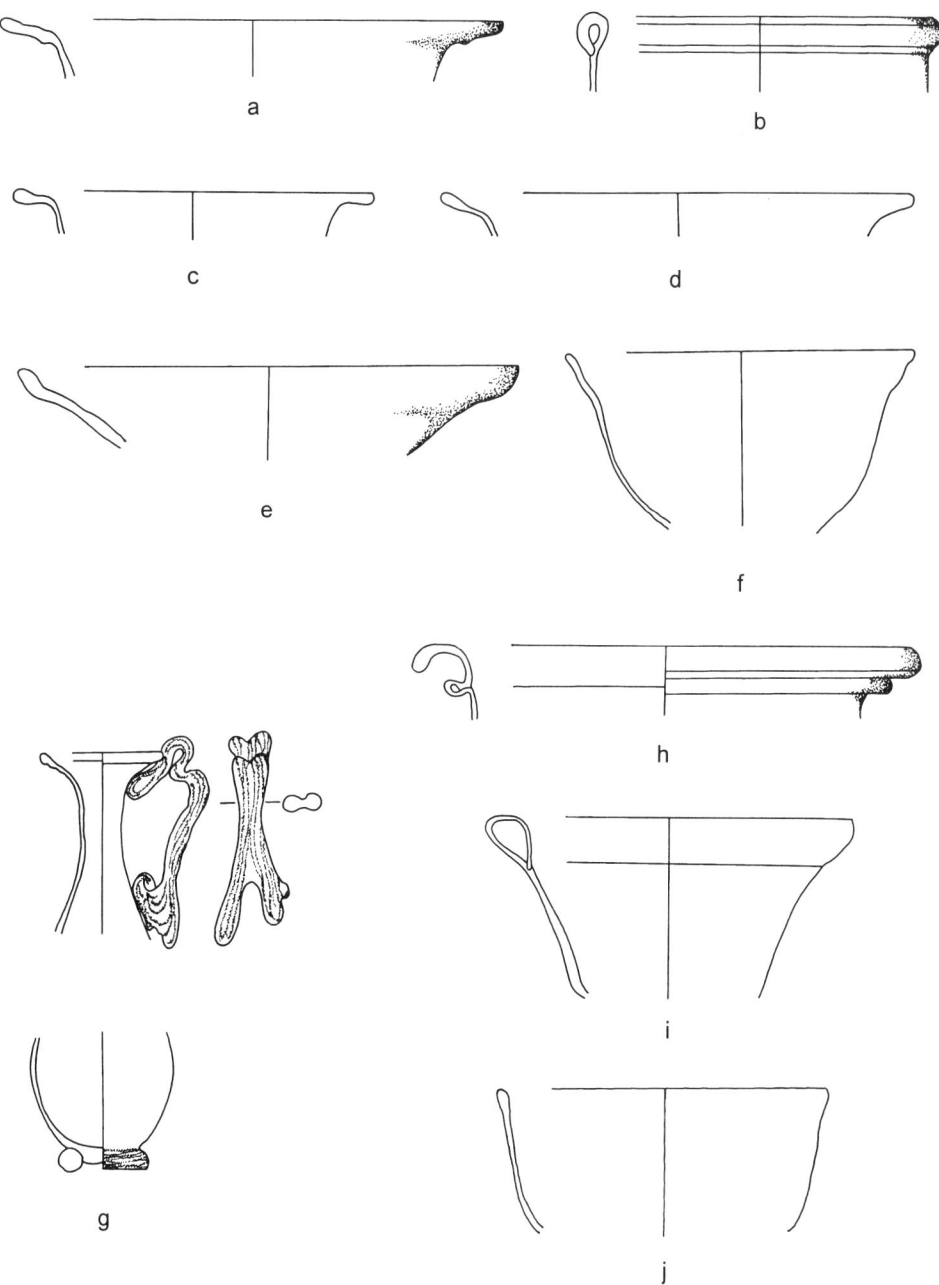

Figure 2 Glass from House 4, Room N cache. Scale 1:2.

　　　　　　　　　　　　Carla Marchini

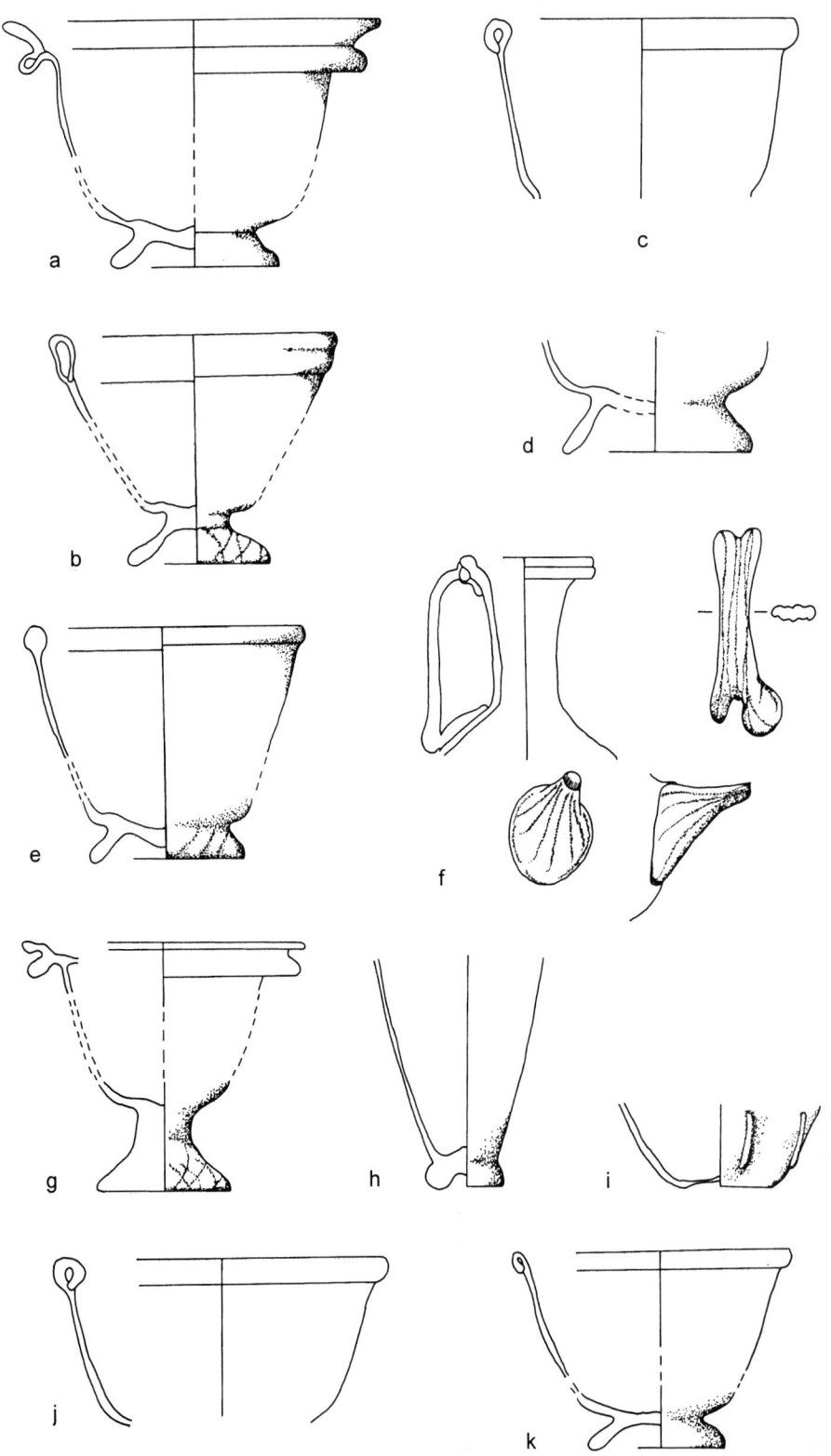

Figure 3 Glass from House 4, Room N cache. Scale 1:2.

29. A/6/321   As 28; not illustrated.
Colour: pale green   Dimensions: Bd = 2.5 cm
Fabric: 1   Harden: III B   Date: IV

30. A/6/322   Figure 3j
Fragments from the rim and body of a deep bowl with outward-folded rim.
Colour: pale green   Dimensions: Bd = 9.6 cm; Ht = 4.6 cm
Fabric: 4   Harden: III A I   Date: IV

31. A/6/323   Figure 3k
Fragmentary deep bowl with plain base ring and outward-folded rim.
Colour: yellow   Dimensions: Rd = 8 cm; Bd = 4.4 cm;
Ht = 5 cm
Fabric: 4   Harden: III A I (a)   Date: IV

Glass from West Tomb 1 and 31/420–C5–2

The glass found in West Tomb 1 (Hope and McKenzie, herein) and in Grave 24 in the cemetery on the east of the settlement, 31/420–C5–2 (Birrell, herein), differs from that found in House 4 and may be ascribed to an earlier date.

The single piece of glass found in 31/420–C5–2/24 is a square bottle. This type is well-known to archaeologists and there exists an extensive literature dealing with them. It may be ascribed to the second–third centuries CE on the basis of comparisons with those studied by Harden (1936, 231) and Charlesworth (1966, 26). The square bottle is a widely-used container from the first century CE onwards; the manufacture of tall square bottles had ceased by the third century (Tatton-Brown 1991, 81). Such vessels were used for the transport and storage of liquids; the shape of the vessel allows efficient storage without waste of space and better protection from breakage. The thickness and quality of the glass helps to confirm this hypothesis; the square bottles are usually made of thick, bubbly glass of a dark green or blue-green colour that was highly resistant and at the same time inexpensive. This could well explain the widespread use of square bottles throughout the Roman world. Sometimes they were used as tableware, but this is not so in the present case; much better quality glass is found within the settlement. Quite often the square bottles were used as cinerary urns or burial equipment as was this example.

The vessel from 31/420–C5–2 grave 24 is free blown and then flattened on the sides;[2] it has rounded corners whereas mould-blown vessels have square corners. This type of vessel was made throughout the Roman world; numerous examples have been found in Italy (de Franciscis 1963), France and Germany etc., and in other more distant regions to where they had probably been imported. The example from 31/420–C5–2 Grave 24 is damaged, lacking its handle, and was undoubtedly reused after this loss.

Of the glass from West Tomb 1, one piece is deserving of comment: the tall-necked flask. This kind of vessel was free-blown and the size varies greatly. There are examples from Karanis which are three centimetres high, and others which are 25 cm high (Harden 1936, 187). We can affirm that they were produced around the second–third centuries CE, as noted by Harden (1936, 186), and we know that they were retained for many years, being a luxury item made of very fine glass. While such vessels might have been used as tableware, within the context of a tomb they were probably used as *ungentaria* or *lacrimaria*. The kind of rim suggests that the vessel would have been used to collect the tears of the relatives of the dead to comfort the deceased in the afterlife. It could also have been used for the storage of precious oils or perfumes.

The Catalogue

The same conventions are employed as in the catalogue of the glass from House 4

1. 31/420–C5–2/24/1   Figure 4a
Square bottle with cylindrical neck and one handle, now missing.
Colour: dark green   Dimensions: Rd = 3.9 cm; Ht = 12 cm;
sides of base 5.3 cm
Fabric: 2   Harden: XI C 1 â   Date: II–III

2. D/7/7   Figure 4b
Tall-necked flask with constricted neck, piriform body and coil base.
Colour: pale green   Dimensions: Rd = 3.3 cm; Ht = 11 cm;
Bd = 3.8 cm.
Fabric: 5   Harden: IX A IV   Date: III

3. D/7/8   Figure 4c
Body of a tall-necked flask with a wide piriform body and indented base.
Colour: transparent   Dimensions: Nd = 1.5 cm; Ht =11 cm;
Bd = 6.7 cm.
Fabric: 5   Harden: IX B I   Date: III

4. D/7/15   Figure 4d
Deep bowl with rounded base and polished plain rim, with incised decoration on the sides.
Colour: deep purple   Dimensions: Rd = 10.2 cm; Ht = 6.5 cm;
Bd = 4.5 cm.
Fabric: 4   Harden: III B II b   Date: III

---

[2] Good parallels to our vessel are: *Ancient Glass. The Bomford Collection of Pre-Roman and Roman Glass on loan to the City of Bristol Museum and Art Gallery*, no. 76; S. Auth, *Ancient Glass at the Newark Museum*, Newark, 1976, no. 128; Tatton-Brown 1991, no. 100.

5. D/7/16   Figure 4e
Deep beaker with polished rim and flat base.
Colour: transparent   Dimensions: Rd = 9.7 cm; Ht = 9.8 cm;
Bd = 3.8 cm.
Fabric: 4   Harden: V A II   Date: III ?

6. D/7/unregistered   Figure 4f
Round base from a deep bowl.
Colour: transparent   Dimensions: Bd = 3.5 cm
Fabric: 4   Harden: III B   Date: III ?

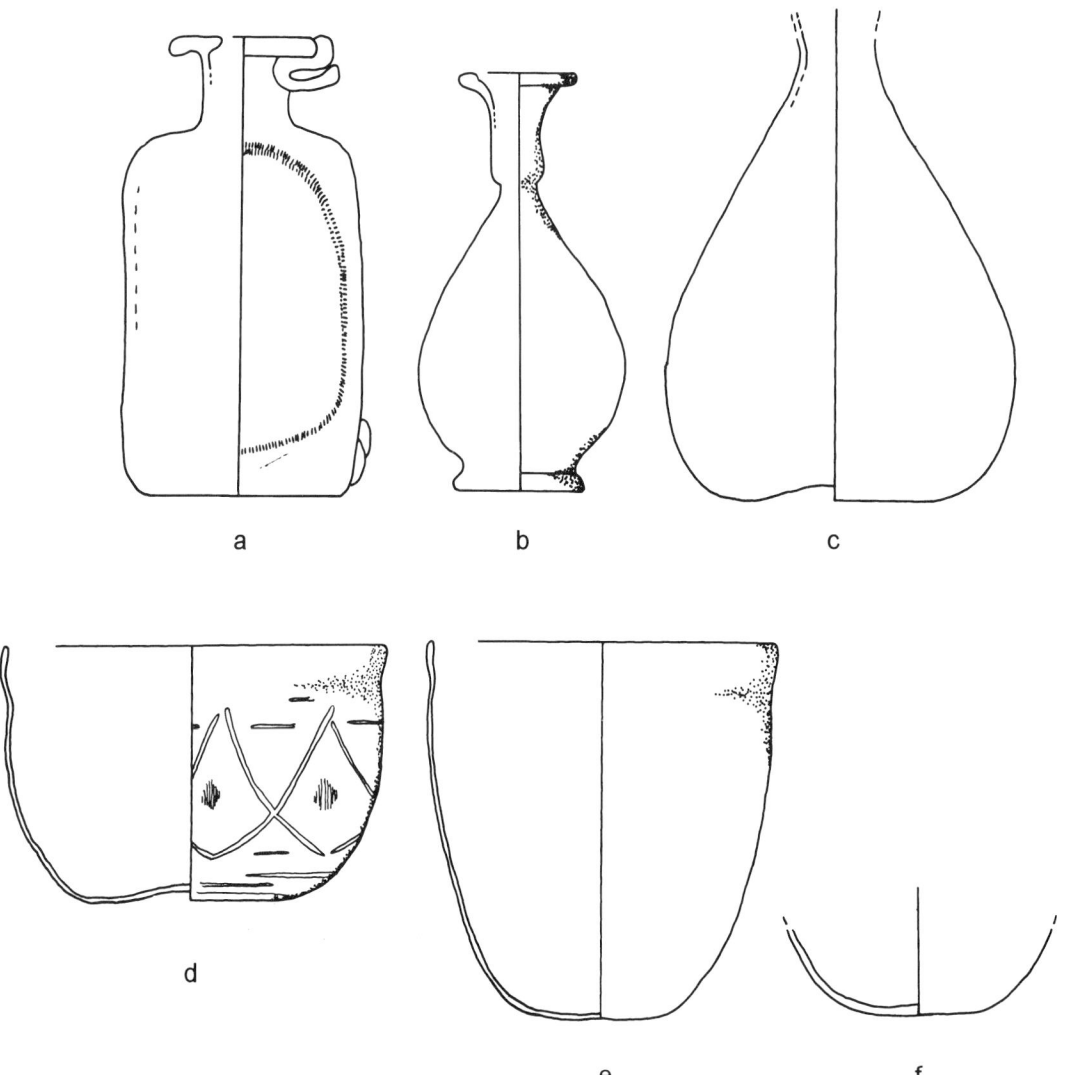

a   b   c

d   e   f

Figure 4 a: Glass vessel from 31/420–C5–2 Grave 24, object 1; b–f: Glass vessels from West Tomb 1, burial chamber.
Scale 1:2.

Report on the Study of the Ceramics:
1993–1994 Seasons

Shirley F. Patten

1993 Season

Work on the pottery from Ismant el-Kharab began in late December 1992 and continued until the middle of February 1993. Priority was given to the recording, reconstruction and drawing of the ceramic material recovered from House 3 and, in particular, to the large number of vessels from Room 6, on which work had commenced in the previous season. At the end of the 1992 season, on completion of the recording of all material from the room, it was calculated that nearly 150 vessels had been stacked in this room at the time the house was abandoned. It was possible to restore over a hundred of the vessels to a complete or near complete condition. All recorded material was drawn. Consequently, with the large number of complete vessels present, it has been possible to make many valuable additions to the corpus of pottery from ancient Kellis.

Excavation of House 4 commenced during the season and a preliminary investigation was undertaken of the ceramic material while it was being recovered from that context. In addition, as work progressed on the Main Temple and Shrine I, pottery from particular contexts was recorded and drawn.[1]

Pottery from House 3, Room 6 (Figure 1)

The pottery from the houses includes a wide variety of types, mostly of a domestic nature. Complete vessels from Room 6 of House 3 range from miniature bowls to very large jars. The majority of the vessels are of local manufacture and the wares are those which are normally encountered at Ismant el-Kharab. The illustrations presented here represent a small number of diagnostic types and wares, and unusual vessels (see also Hope et al. 1989, 20–2; Patten 1993).

Figure 1.1 shows a small bowl exceptional in that the type has not previously been recovered from the domestic context of the houses and it is possible that it is an heirloom. The intact vessel is made from a marl fabric and decorated with dark red rim ticks. The simple open shape with a ring base is well made.

Figure 1.2 illustrates one example of the many types of small bowls recovered from the room. The moderately hard-fired, dense fabric is one which was often used in the manufacture of domestic vessels; the fired colour is generally pink to grey. Rim decoration of red ticks, as on this thinly-potted bowl, is typical. The fabric is used commonly for restricted forms, but also for large open bowls with ledge rims decorated with red bars. As rim sherds in this fabric are very numerous amongst excavated material, the large number of complete bowls recovered here will facilitate identification and processing.

The bowl-shaped funnel (Figure 1.3) was made from another fabric also utilized in the fourth century CE for many different types of vessel. The iron-bearing clay of this fabric is fired red-brown in oxidising atmospheres and grey in reducing atmospheres, designated currently as A1a and A1b respectively. The texture of the fabric is moderately open with rounded quartz and white calcareous inclusions which are usually numerous and conspicuous. The rim of the funnel is decorated with red bars.

Figure 1.4 is one of the small jars recovered; although intact, it is fairly certain that the fabric is A1a. It is well made and the form is new to the corpus. The large flask (Figure 1.5) was made from a shale-tempered fabric which, judging by the material so far recovered from the houses, was used particularly for such vessels and open bowls of medium size. Both forms are regularly decorated, the bowls in monochrome brown on the interior with spirals on their bases and sides, and the flasks in bichrome

---

[1] For a brief report on these excavations see Bowen et al. 1993.

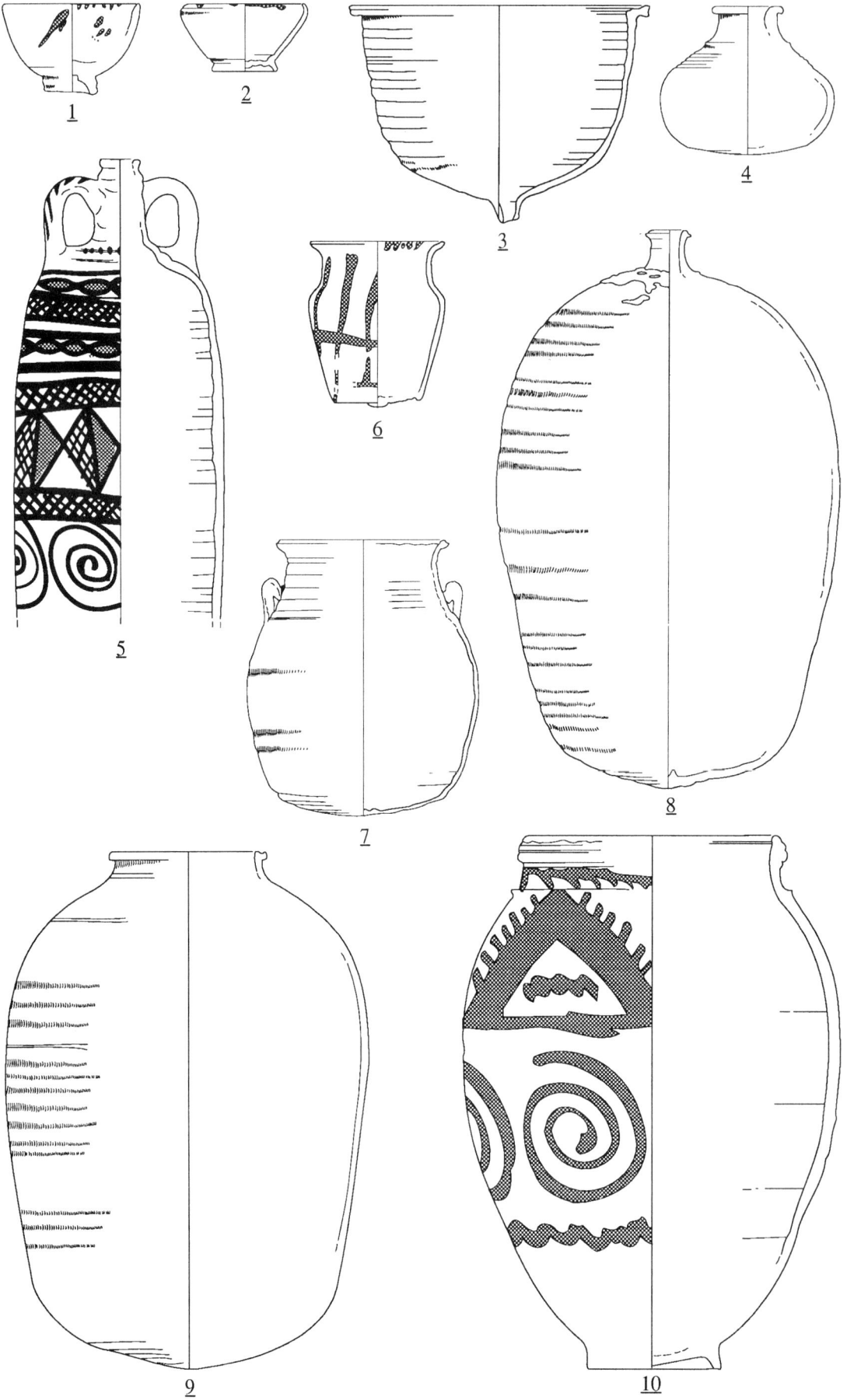

Figure 1 Pottery from Area A: House 3, Room 6. 1–7 scale 1:4 and 8–10; Scale 1:5.

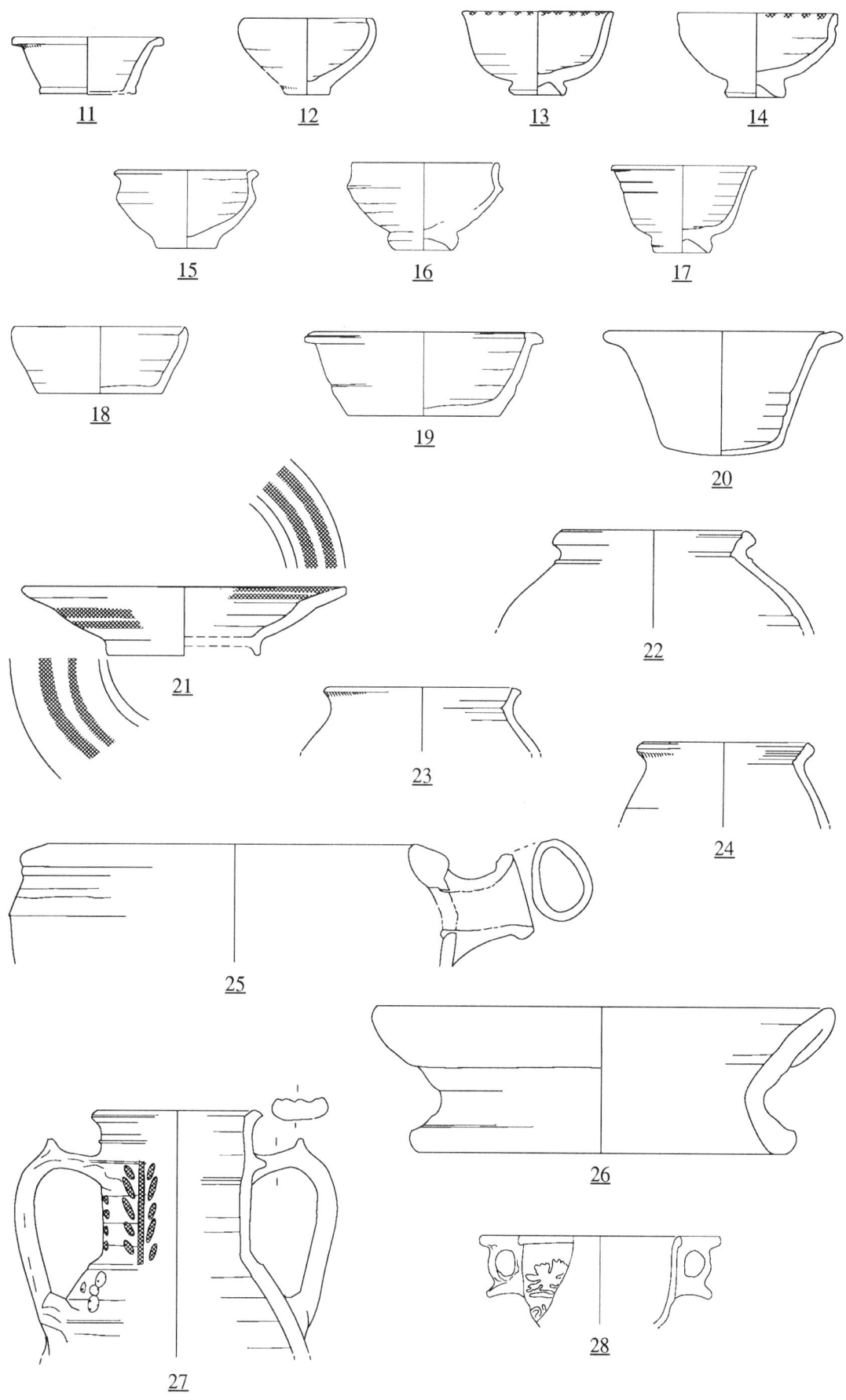

Figure 2 11–26: Pottery from early levels in Areas A and B, except 16 which is from Area D; Scale 1:4.
27–28: Vessels from Deir el-Haggar; Scale 1:4.

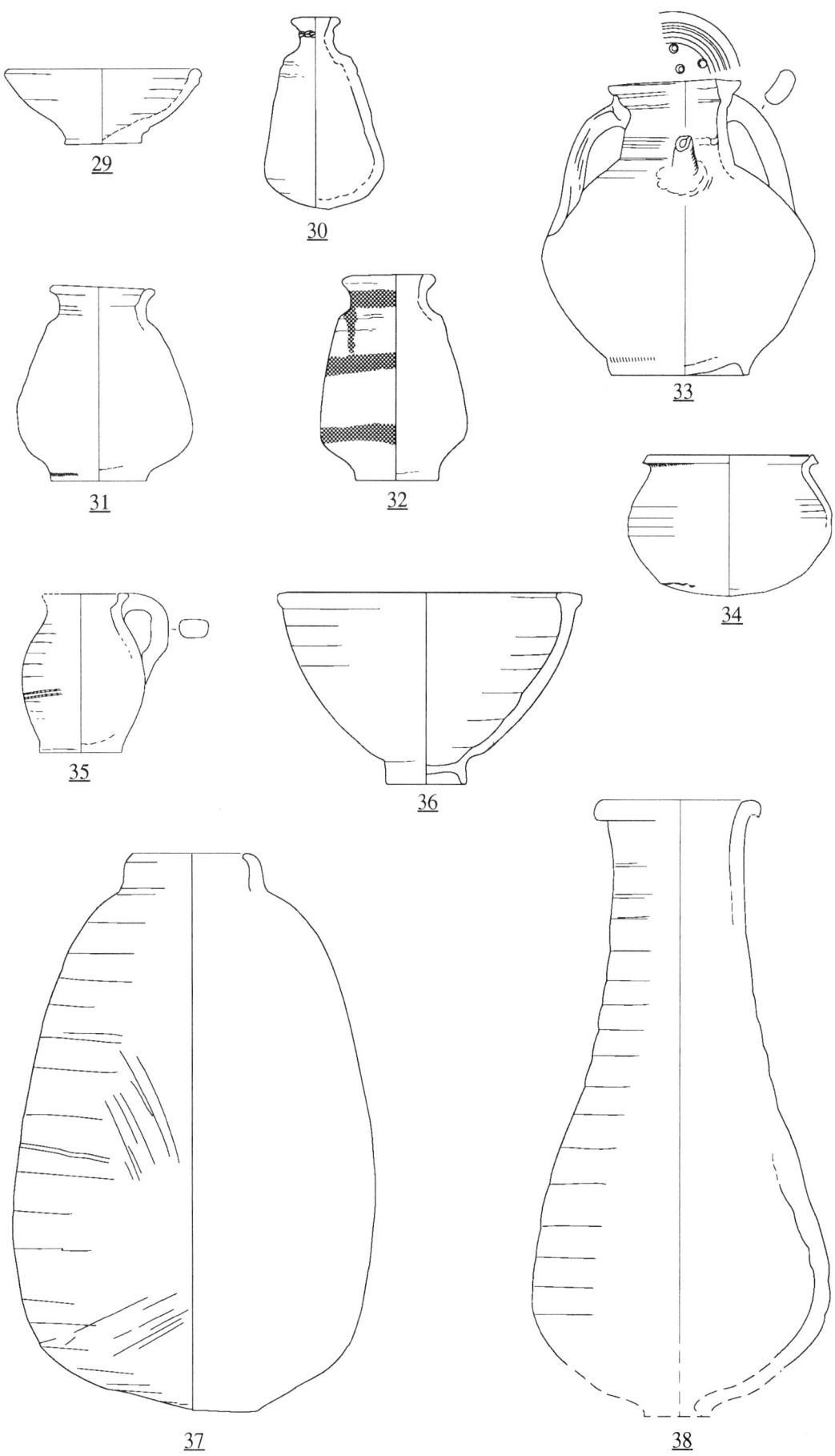

*Figure 3 Pottery from the cemeteries of Ismant el-Kharab: 29–37 from 31/420–C5–1
and 38 from 31/420–C5–2; 29–36 Scale 1:4 and 37–38 Scale 1:5.*

red and brown on the exterior with motifs typified by this example.

Figure 1.6 illustrates one of three similar small jars from Room 6. The fabric is a marl with open, porous texture; the fired colour is cream to pale green. Vessels in this fabric are quite light in weight. The same fabric was frequently used for globular and lentoid flasks.

Cooking vessels are well represented in the sherd material and it was possible to restore a large number. Figure 1.7 shows one of the smaller examples which is made in the same fabric as the bowl of Figure 1.2. Although this fabric is quite dense it must have withstood thermal shock well, as it was the fabric used most frequently for cooking vessels, large and small.

The large jar (Figure 1.8) is the only example of the type recovered so far at the site and it is not represented amongst material discovered during the survey of the oasis. The narrow neck was thrown separately and luted onto the body. Plaster from the sealing still adheres to the neck and upper body. The jar shown in Figure 1.9 is one of two almost identical vessels, and these are the only examples from the excavations at Ismant el-Kharab to date. Sherds from large decorated jars frequently occur in the excavated material. Figure 1.10 depicts one of four complete examples discovered in Houses 3 and 4. The decoration is executed in a dark red-brown pigment casually applied over a cream slip. Motifs painted on the jars include palm branches, spirals, crosses, bands and wavy lines.

1994 Season

Work on the ceramics commenced in early January 1994 and a summary reported elsewhere (Patten 1996). The primary focus of the season was the recording and drawing of the ceramic material excavated from well-stratified contexts in Houses 3 and 4 during the previous two seasons. The pottery found in the cemeteries situated a short distance to the north-west and the north-east of Ismant el-Kharab (Birrell, herein) was also recorded and drawn. In addition, a preliminary investigation of the material from the Dakhleh Oasis Project's work at Deir el-Haggar (Mills, herein) was undertaken.

House 3 is the most easterly of the group of three excavated houses. The group is situated to the south of the large civic building of Area B, parts of which were excavated in 1988, from which it is separated by a street. The courtyard of House 3 was built adjoining the northern side of the house, and excavations below floor level in the structures against the north wall of the courtyard produced sherd material similar to that recovered in the lower levels of the Area B excavations (Hope 1987, 167–72, Figure 5).

In general, the ceramic material recovered from the excavation of House 4 is similar to that from the habitation levels of Houses 1–3. On examination of fill material

from under the floors of one of the rooms, however, it was found that sherds from the context were comparable with those from the lower levels of the courtyard of House 3 and Area B. Consequently, we now have ceramics from three well-stratified contexts which pre-date the main occupation phase of the houses. The excavated material from this earlier period is invaluable in that it establishes a chronological sequence for the site and also enables the dating of material discovered during the survey of the oasis.

The sherds recovered from the three contexts comprise a wide range of domestic vessels. Large and small bowls, cooking vessels and jars are the most common. The majority are made from the reddish brown-fired fabric A1a described above, which was used extensively in the period of occupation of the houses (late III–IV CE). Another range of fabrics from this earlier period was made from marl clay, generally fired cream to pink, and denser and harder than the marl fabrics of the later period. Two fabrics which typify the later period, the thinly-thrown, pinkish-grey fabric and the red-slipped and polished ware which imitated North African Red Slip wares, are noticeably absent in the earlier levels.

Pottery from the Project's work at Deir el-Haggar provides numerous parallels to that from the earlier contexts at Ismant el-Kharab, and assists in assigning a date to the latter within the early Roman Period (I–II CE).

Ceramics from Early Contexts

Figure 2.11–17 illustrate a range of small bowls from several of the contexts. No. 13 (House 4) and No. 16 (Shrine I of the Main Temple complex) are made from marl fabrics and are decorated with red rim ticks. The larger bowls (fig. 2.18–20) are from House 3. Figure 2.18 has a parallel in the material from Dush in Khargeh Oasis; the third century CE date suggested for the piece may be a little late (Ballet 1990, 299–301, Figure 5). Figure 2.21, also from House 3, is decorated with painted bands in dark red paint on the interior and exterior; it is the only example discovered to date. Cooking vessels from the earlier levels differ from those of the later not only in fabric but also in shape, as can be seen from a comparison of Figures 2.22–24 with Figure 1.7.

In Dakhleh Oasis, spouted vessels are frequently encountered in material of different periods, but Figure 2.25 is unique amongst the material excavated as yet at Ismant el-Kharab. A similar vessel, however, was one of a group of vessels recovered during the survey of the oasis (Hope 1981, Plates XXVIIk, XXXIa). The sherd comes from House 3 and is made in A1a fabric with a cream slip. Though heavily potted, the vessel is well made with a thickened rim and an applied spout. The potstand, Figure 2.26, is made in the same fabric and was recovered from the same context.

Ceramics from Deir el-Haggar

Only two of the most interesting pieces are illustrated
here. The sherds reconstructed to form the neck and upper
body of a two-handled amphora, Figure 2.27, derive from
work within the temple. The neck is decorated with a
plant motif in dark red and there are horizontal bars of the
same colour on the handle above and below the thumb
boss. The decoration is continued on the body but the
motif is difficult to identify. Figure 2.28, a sherd from a
red-ware skyphos, may be dated to the first century BCE
– first century CE; it is a surface find. It is interesting that
two sherds from a similar vessel, the only other discovered
so far, were recovered from the surface of a neighbouring
site during the survey (Hope, in press b).

The Cemeteries of Ismant el-Kharab

The vessels illustrated in Figure 3.29–37 derive from
excavations within 31/420–C5–1, located west of the
settlement, and Figure 3.38 comes from 31/420–C5–2
east of the settlement (for both see Birrell, herein).

Vessels in Figure 3.29–32 come from Tomb 13. The
four vessels were all made from fabric A1a. Jars similar
to those of Figure 3.31–32 were recovered from various
cemeteries during the survey of the oasis (Hope 1980,
Plates XXIIIa, m, XXIVc; 1981, Plate XXVIl-o, XXXc).
The small flask, Figure 3.30, which was used as a container
for oil or resin, has a thin cord tied around its neck and
was closed with a sealing; it has a thick red coating. The
vessels from Tomb 13 indicate that the cemetery may

have been in use earlier than previously thought, possibly
at least as early as the Ptolemaic Period. Figure 3.33,
from outside Tomb 1, is made from the pale cream marl
fabric. There are a number of good parallels for Figure
3.33 dated to around the first and second centuries CE; a
similar, but larger, vessel was recovered in the group that
contained a parallel to the spouted bowl Figure 2.25 (Hope
1981, Plates XXVIIi, XXXIb). The restricted bowl Figure
3.34 is from the fill of the same tomb; the A1a fabric of
this bowl is soft as if under-fired. The handled jug Figure
3.35 is from Tomb 2. The bowl of Figure 3.36, a surface
find, is well made from A1a fabric and evenly fired a pale
red colour. The intact large jar from Tomb 9, figure 3.37,
has a small fibre bung filling a hole in its upper body; the
fabric is almost certainly a fine variant of A1a. Rim sherds
from types similar to both the latter two occur frequently
amongst the earlier material in the settlement; bowls of
this type became much larger in the occupation phase of
the houses.

Figure 3.38 is an example of the commonest type of
vessel found in the graves of the cemetery east of the site,
31/420–C5–2. These large vessels, termed 'pigeon pots',
have a purposely-made hole in the base. Similar vessels
were recovered from sites in the western part of the oasis
during the survey, predominantly farmhouses (*columbaria*)
(Hope 1979, 194–5, Plate XIX.11). They occur at Ismant
el-Kharab in association with one such building on the
extreme north of the site. In this cemetery the type is
mostly attested by fragmentary examples which have
clearly been reused (Birrell, herein Plate 10).

Plant Remains from Kellis: First Results

Ursula Thanheiser[1]

Preservation of plant remains at Kellis is excellent. Most of them are desiccated, only a small proportion has been charred.

So far five different types of archaeological plant assemblages have been recovered:

a) floral bouquets from graves
b) hand-picked plant remains from various areas of the excavation
c) plant remains in soil samples from house floors
d) temper in mud bricks
e) pillow stuffing (not yet analysed)

Floral bouquets from graves

From the abundance of floral bouquets recovered so far, only one has been analysed. This derives from the northeast corner of the burial chamber in West Tomb 1 (Hope and McKenzie, herein). It consists of myrtle twigs (*Myrtus communis*) tied together with grass leaves (*cf. Desmostachya bipinnata*). Rosemary leaves (*Rosmarinus officinalis*) are trapped between the myrtle twigs.

Hand-picked plant remains

During the excavation, large fruits/seeds were collected from various areas of the site. To obtain a general view of the recovered taxa, 19 samples have been chosen randomly and the results of the analysis are presented in Table 1.[2] For obvious reasons, the composition of the samples is biased as only rather large fruits/seed can actually be seen in the soil during the excavation.

Soil samples

Soil samples were taken from House 4. The plant remains were retrieved by using an electrostatic device and identified under a microscope with the help of the writer's modern reference collection of fruit/seed and plant collections at the Institute of Botany, Vienna University. Several types of plant remains have been recovered: cereals, pulses, fibre plants, fruit, vegetable and spices, herbaceous plants, trees and shrubs. Detailed results of the analysis are given in Table 2.

Temper in mud bricks

For mud-brick temper, the chaff of barley (*Hordeum vulgare*) was widely used. Rachis fragments and sterile lateral florets of two-rowed barley (*Hordeum vulgare ssp. distichum*) predominate.

Discussion

Cereals

The remains of three cereal crops were found at Kellis: bread wheat (*Triticum aestivum*), two-rowed barley (*Hordeum vulgare ssp. distichum*) and six-rowed barley (*Hordeum vulgare ssp. vulgare*). Bread wheat and barley occur in more or less equal proportions. For both cereals, chaff (rachis fragments, glumes, hulls, sterile lateral florets) predominate. No cereal crops of African origin (sorghum or millets) have been found.

Barley was amongst the earliest cereals cultivated in

---

[1] Instiut für Botanik der Universität Wien, Rennweg 14, A-1030 Vienna, Austria.

[2] The samples have been analysed at the site where no microscope was available. Therefore, there is a rather large number of taxa which could not be identified to species level although the state of preservation is very good. More hand-picked samples from Kellis have been analysed by Ritchie (in press). In addition to the taxa listed in Table 1, he found myrtle leaf and twig fragments (*Myrtus sp.*), charcoal from tamarisk (*Tamarix sp.*), willow (Salix sp.), *Sesbania sp.* and reed (*Typha sp.*).

Table 1 Hand-picked Samples.

Sample No.	P1	P2	P3	P4	P5	P6	P7	P8	P9
Prunus armeniaca	1	-	-	-	-	-	-	-	-
Prunus persica	-	1	-	1	1	-	1	4	1
Punica granatum	-	-	1	-	-	2	1	-	-
Cucurbitaceae	-	-	-	-	-	-	-	-	2
Olea europaea	2	9	23	1	21	1	1	10	5
Zizyphus spina-christi	-	-	-	-	-	-	-	-	15
Phoenix dactylifera	19	*79	10	3	8	112	-	192	99
Hyphaene thebaica	-	-	-	2	-	-	-	-	-

Sample No.	P10	P11	P12	P13	P14	P15	P16	P17	P18	P19
Triticum sp.	-	-	-	7	-	13	-	16	1	1
Hordeum vulgare	-	-	-	42	-	18	-	6	30	1
Juglans regia	1	1	-	-	-	-	-	-	-	-
Prunus persica	1	-	1	-	-	-	1	1	-	-
Vicia faba	-	-	4	-	-	-	1	1	-	4
Fabaceae	-	-	-	13	-	30	-	-	-	-
Cucurbitaceae	-	-	-	4	1	5	-	-	6	10
Vitis vinifera ssp. vinifera	-	-	-	~800	1	94	3	6	10	~300
Zizyphus spina-christi	18	15	12	5	7	6	1	3	2	11
Gossypium sp	-	-	-	-	-	20	-	-	-	-
Phoenix dactylifera	~300	~400	~1300	-	~300	-	-	6	-	-
Hyphaene thebaica	1	-	2	-	-	-	1	1	1	-

* Both desiccated and charred specimen are present.

Provenance of Samples

	Provenance		Excavation Sample No.
P1	31/420-D6-1/A/4	Deposit 8	87.147
P2	31/420-D6-1/A/4	Deposit 9	87.154
P3	31/420-D6-1/A/1	Room 1 Deposit 3	87.003
P4	31/420-D6-1/A/1	Room 9 Deposit 4	87.066
P5	31/420-D6-1/A/1	Room 11 Deposit 2	87.095
P6	31/420-D6-1/A/2	Room 9 Deposit 5	89.017
P7	31/420-D6-1/A/2	Room 1 Deposit 5	87.307
P8	31/420-D6-1/A/3	Room 1 Deposit 6	87.026
P9	31/420-D6-1/B/1	Room 1, Test 1	89.096
P10	31/420-D6-1/D/IB	Deposit 7	92.033
P11	31/420-D6-1/D/1B	Deposit 8	92.036
P12	31/420-D6-1/D/1B	Deposit 9	92.042
P13	31/420-D6-1/D/1B	Deposit 9	92.048
P14	31/420-D6-1/D/1B	Deposit 10	92.052
P15	31/420-D6-1/D/1B	Deposit 10	92.053
P16	31/420-D6-1/D/1B	Deposit 14	92.089
P17	31/420-D6-1/D/1B	Deposit 15	92.091
P18	31/420-D6-1/D/1B	Deposit 16	92.097
P19	31/420 D6-1/D/1B	Deposit 17	92.102

the Near East and remained one of the principal crops during the prehistoric period. It made its first appearance in Egypt in the Fayum and at Merimde shortly after 6000 bp (Caton-Thompson and Gardner 1934, 46ff.; Hassan 1988, 151). Free-threshing wheat[3] (*Triticum durum, T. aestivum*) came into cultivation in the Near East not much later than barley but seems to have been of secondary importance initially. Only by the beginning of the first millennium BC many of the Near Eastern and Mediterranean sites show a prevalence of free-threshing wheats (Zohary and Hopf 1988, 36). It is commonly held that in Egypt the replacement of emmer wheat (*T. dicoccum*), one of the staple crops of pharaonic times, started during the Ptolemaic period (Germer 1985, 213). Bread wheat is a more demanding crop to grow than either emmer or barley, but due to its high gluten contents has better bread-making qualities. Why macaroni-wheat (*T. durum*) was not widely cultivated in Egypt although it is better adapted to Mediterranean climate than bread wheat is unknown.

It is interesting to note that so far no remains of einkorn (*Triticum monococcum*) have been found at Kellis. The 'Kellis Agricultural Account Book' recovered from House 2 in 1988 (Bagnall 1997; Bagnall et al, 1998) mentions several units of τιφαγιον (tiphagion), i.e. something made of τιφη (tiph). Wagner (1990) translated τιφη as being einkorn and justifies this translation by etymological reasoning. Percival (1974, 171) states that τιφη mentioned by ancient Greek authors seems to be the name for einkorn.

Einkorn is a primitive wheat and has its centre of origin in the fertile crescent. It was widely cultivated during the Neolithic in the Near East and in Europe. Since the Bronze Age its importance seems to have declined gradually and today it is a relic crop. Einkorn is adapted to cold winters and does badly under irrigation. There is neither archaeological evidence nor are there any written accounts other than the 'Kellis Agricultural Account Book' in Egypt and adjacent African countries which would justify the assumption of its cultivation in Dakhleh. The few grains of einkorn found on various Egyptian sites were either misidentified[4] or are thought to have grown as weeds in other cereal crops (Barakat 1990, 109–10; Thanheiser in press).

Pulses

Only a few seeds but numerous testa fragments of a small seeded variety of broad bean (*Vicia faba ssp. paucijuga*) were found. Some of them had the hilum still attached. Identification was possible with the aid of a scanning electron microscope and Ann Butler's outstanding expertise in testa morphology of *Vicieae*.[5]

Today the broad bean is one of Egypt's staple crops, a status which it presumably also held in previous times.

Pulses are attractive because, in contrast to most other flowering plants, they are able to fix atmospheric nitrogen through symbiosis with the root bacterium *Rhizobium*. Therefore, pulses add nitrogen to the soil rather than using it up. By field rotation or by mixing pulse crops with cereals the farmer is able to maintain a higher level of soil fertility. Pulses are extremely rich in proteins and therefore complement cereals, the principal source of carbohydrates, in the diet.

Fibre Plants

Only few remains of flax capsules (*Linum sp.*) and cotton seeds (*Gossypium sp.*) have been found. While flax was known in Egypt since predynastic times (Lucas 1962, 142–6), cotton is a latecomer, making its first appearance in Roman contexts at Qasr Ibrim (Crowfoot 1979, 40; Lucas 1962, 147–8)

Fruits

The recovered taxa comprise a large variety of fruit collected from the wild, indigenous cultivated plants, cultivated plants of foreign origin and imported ones.

This group is clearly dominated by the remains of date (*Phoenix dactylifera*). More than 2,800 stones, some of them charred, were found. Date palms are a characteristic plant of desert oases. Their importance, both as food and building material, since very early times is clearly demonstrated by numerous archaeological finds (Täckholm and Drar 1950, 218ff) and an abundance of pictorial representations (Wallert 1962).

Apricot (*Prunus armeniaca*), peach (*P. persica*), pomegranate (*Punica granatum*), grape (*Vitis vinifera ssp. vinifera*) and olive (*Olea europaea*) are not native to Egypt. They originate in the Near East (Zohary and Hopf 1988) and came into cultivation in Egypt in different periods.

Grapes have been known in Egypt since predynastic times. Important areas of cultivation were the Nile Delta, the Fayum, Kharga and Dakhleh Oasis (Kees 1955, 41).

Pomegranate and olive were first imported during the Second Intermediate Period and the oldest archaeological finds so far come from Tell el-Dab'a (Thanheiser, in press). From the New Kingdom onwards they have been cultivated in Egypt.

---

[3] Until recently the archaeological remains of free-threshing wheat could not be distinguished from one another (cf. van Zeist 1983, 53).

[4] The finds of einkorn in el-Omari (Debono 1948, 568), in King Djoser's pyramid and Queen Icheti's tomb (Tackholm 1951, 127–8) were later re-identified as being emmer (Helbaek 1953, 7; Schiemann 1954, 146).

[5] I wish to thank A. Butler, Institute of Archaeology, University College London, for the effort she took identifying the testa fragments.

Table 2 Soil Samples.

Sample No.	P1	P2	P3	P4	P5
Amount of Soil Sampled (Litre)	1.6	1.6	1.1	1.6	1.4
Items per Litre	293	338	178	109	199
Triticum aestivum rachis fragment	17	57	15	3	24
Triticum aestivum glume	6	-	-	-	5
Triticum aestivum	-	1	-	-	-
Triticum sp. rachis fragment	-	6	-	-	1
Triticum sp. glume	-	-	2	-	11
Hordeum vulgare ssp. distichum rachis fragment	*16	15	6	1	9
Hordeum vulgare ssp. distichum sterile floret	8	4	1	2	-
Hordeum vulgare ssp. vulgare rachis fragment	*14	12	5	1	5
Hordeum vulgare rachis fragment	*30	25	8	3	10
Hordeum vulgare basal rachis fragment	-	1	1	-	-
Hordeum vulgare hull	-	-	-	1	-
Hordeum vulgare symmetric/hulled	-	7	2	-	-
Cereals indet. rachis fragment	-	-	-	1	-
Cereals indet. glume	11	11	-	2	-
Viciafaba ssp. paucyuga testa	2	36	10	36	2
Linum sp. capsule	4	-	2	-	-
Gossypium sp.	-	-	-	1	1
Pinus pinea	-	-	3	5	1
Prunus persica	-	-	-	-	1
Punica granatum	-	-	-	-	1
Vitis vinifera ssp. vinifera stalk	-	2	-	-	-
Vitis vinifera ssp. vinifera	35	32	20	39	91
Zizyphus spina-christi	!4	2	2	5	2
Ficus carica	*120	29	37	*39	56
Olea europaea	*2	2	-	5	-
Phoenix dactylifera stalk	1	5	3	1	-
Phoenix dactylifera	2	15	2	-	-
Coryandrum sativum	7	8	1	1	1
Apium cf. graveolens	7	3	11	1	-
cf *Pimpinella anisum*	-	-	1	1	-
Medicagol/Melilotus sp.	-	-	-	-	3
Coronilla-type	-	1	-	-	-
Trifolium-type	!7	-	-	-	-
Fabaceae indet.	-	-	-	!1	-
cf. *Myrtus communis* leaf	-	4	4	1	-
Apium cf. nodiflorum	-	-	3	-	-
Angelica-type	-	-	1	-	-
Apiaceae indet.	-	-	-	-	1
Tamarix nilotica twig	-	98	10	3	1
Dicotyledonae indet. leaf	-	-	7	-	-
Carex sp.	-	-	1	-	2
Schoenoplectus sp.	-	-	-	-	1
Cyperaceae indet.	-	-	-	1	-
Sphaenopus sp. infloreseense	7	-	-	-	1
Sample No.	P1	P2	P3	P4	P5
Cutandia cf. divaricata infloreseense	7	-	-	-	3
Avena cf. fatua floret	-	1	-	-	2
Poaceae subtribe *Triticeae*	-	2	-	-	-
Setaria cf. italica	-	1	-	-	-
cf. *Pennisetum sp.* inflorescense	12	76	32	16	41
Poaceae subtribe *Paniceae*	-	-	-	2	-
Poaceae indet. rachis fragment	2	21	6	1	3
Poaceae indet.	-	1	-	-	-
INDET	*52	9	-	1	4

When not stated otherwise the recovered items are fruit/seed.
* Both charred and desiccated specimen are present.   ! Only charred specimen are present.

Provenance of Samples

	Provenance		Excavation Sample No.
P1	31/420-D6-1/A/6	Room 5B Deposit 2A	93.261
P2	31/420-D6-1/A/6	Room 4 Deposit 2	93.263
P3	31/420-D6-1/A/6	Room 6 Deposit 6	93.324
P4	31/420-D6-1/A/6	Room 6 Deposit 7	93.327
P5	31/420-D6-1/A/6	Room 6 Deposit 9	93.328

Apricot and peach were the latest newcomers. Originating in China, they reached Egypt during the Ptolemaic period (Germer 1985, 60–1).

Pine cones (*Pinus pinea*) and walnuts (*Juglans regia*) were imported, presumably for their delicious seeds, since the 12th Dynasty (Täckholm and Täckholm 1941, 70f.) and the Roman period (Germer 1985, 21) respectively. Although planted in gardens, the trees have never become naturalised in Egypt.

Vegetable and Spices

Ancient Egyptians seem to have been as proud of their gardens as their modern descendants. Here they grew ornamentals as well as vegetable, fruit, spices and drugs.

Celery (*Apium cf. graveolens*) grows wild in Africa, Europe and the Americas. Besides being a delicious vegetable and salad plant, it is a tonic, an appetiser and a carminative. The fresh juice is diuretic. Celery grows in Egyptian gardens today as it did in pharaonic times, at least from the end of the New Kingdom. Its leaves were also used for garlands (Schweinfurth 1887, 13).

All recovered spices like anis (*Pimpinella anisum*), coriander (*Coriandrum sativum*) and rosemary (*Rosmarinus officinalis*) are not native to Egypt. They originate in the eastern Mediterranean region and appeared in Egypt from the 18th Dynasty onwards (Germer 1985, 135ff.).

Herbaceous plants and trees

Myrtle (*Myrtus communis*), a component of Mediterranean macchia vegetation, has been grown in Egyptian gardens since the Ptolemaic period. From that time garlands and bouquets have been found (Keimer 1924, 46).

Eighteen taxa of herbaceous plants have been identified. The commonest were parts of the inflorescence of a grass, cf. *Pennisetum sp.*, and unidentifiable rachis fragments of grass, *Poaceae* indet.

Conclusions

The aim of the initial analysis of plant remains from Kellis was an assessment of the potential for further research. Plant remains proved to occur in excellent condition and high concentrations. Therefore further archaeobotanical work will not only give information concerning the plant remains, but also on harvesting methods and crop processing techniques. A detailed analysis of the distribution of desiccated plant remains may yield information on site formation processes.

A Painted Panel of Isis

Helen Whitehouse
with a note by Colin Hope

The Find Context

The painted panel with a depiction of Isis was found during the short season of excavations conducted between 29th January and 10th February in 1994.[1] It was discovered in the north-west corner of Room 3 of the Main Temple of Tutu.[2]

The excavation of this room commenced in 1991 when it was cleared of surface sand, and stone and brick collapse resulting from the dismantling of the temple. Under this rubble was a layer of brown sand with chaff, reaching a maximum depth of 25 cm, which contained an abundance of mostly very small fragments of papyrus inscribed in Greek and Demotic, and fragments from at least one gilded, wooden barque shrine decorated with the figures of various deities flanked by either standing or kneeling goddesses with wings outstretched. Other fragments were found in the court to the east, along with fragments of plaster and stone sculptures.[3] Beneath this material was loose, brown powdery earth overlying compacted earth floors. These were of irregular depth across the room; they were almost level with the door sills into Rooms 2 and 4, to the west and east of Room 3 respectively, and banked up considerably against the north and south walls of the room. The floors were not well preserved and in the centre the stone paving of the room was exposed.

In 1992 the examination of the earth floors commenced. Resulting from the poor state of preservation it was not possible to isolate individual floor levels. This revealed what appeared to be pits filled with earth material in the north-eastern and north-western corners of the room. Work in the room was continued in 1994 (Plate 1) with the aim of exposing the original floor of the room and those of the corridors to its north and south and the court to its east. This resulted in the immediate discovery of the painted panel lying face upwards.

The piece was found 27 cm below the preserved top of the western wall, which is actually its foundation course, in the north-western corner of the room. It lay against this wall, 13 cm from the northern wall and had been buried in the earth floor material to a depth of 22 cm. The level at which it was discovered coincides with that of the stone paving of the room. While paving blocks were revealed over most of the room, those from the northern corners were missing (Plate 2). As was indicated elsewhere in the room, the stone paving underwent much wear before the earth floors accumulated, but it would seem that the corner slabs had been removed deliberately. This exposed deposits of small pieces of sandstone between larger pieces upon the Nubian basal clay; this material is part of a sandstone platform upon which Room 3 was built. The platform was also encountered in excavations within the corridor north of Room 3 (Plate 2) and in the court to its east.[4] The pits formed by the removal of the paving slabs subsequently filled with the same earthy material of which the floors consisted.

Thus, the Isis panel was lost after the damage to the

---

[1] The 1994 field season at Ismant el-Kharab was primarily a study season funded by the Egyptology Society of Victoria (Monash University) and donations from individual members of the society; the Rosemary and Eric Cromby Travel Scholarship again enabled a senior student from Monash University to participate in the work. I am particularly grateful to all who made the season possible.

[2] For the location of this room see the plan published in Figure 3 of Hope et al. 1989.

[3] For a discussion of the excavations and illustrations of several of the objects see the article cited in the previous note.

[4] This does not appear to represent foundation for the temple. It has an alignment which differs from that of the temple and associated with it were architectural fragments which indicate that it is the remains of an earlier formal structure.

Plate 1 Main Temple, Room 3, with earth floors in 1994, looking south-west.

Plate 2 Main Temple, Room 3 and North Corridor, looking south, showing broken pavement in the northern part of Room 3 and part of the stone platform revealed in the North Corridor.

paved floor of the room had occurred but at the beginning of the period which saw the build-up of the earth floors. Current evidence would indicate that the temple was constructed between the mid-first and mid-second centuries CE, with some minor additions at the end of the second century and into the third century. There is no evidence to date precisely when the stone paving in Room 3 might have been damaged nor over what duration of time the earth floors were laid. Documentary evidence shows that a priest of Tutu and his consort Tapsais, named Aurelios Stonios, was still in office in 335 (Worp 1995, no. 13). Sometime before the abandonment of the site at the end of the fourth century the temple witnessed domestic activity and parts were used as refuse dumps. Hence, it may be suggested tentatively that the earth floors accumulated during such activity and that the Isis panel was lost in approximately the mid-fourth century. Ceramic material found in the floors would support this idea.

(CAH)

The Painted Panel

The painted panel (Plate 3) is an important addition to the meagre number of excavated examples of such depictions so far recorded. Despite its comparatively poor state of preservation, the quality of the picture, a bust-length portrait of the goddess Isis in Graeco-Roman style, is striking; when freshly painted, the panel must have presented a delicate and quite finely-detailed representation of the goddess, shown as a more youthful and charming figure than the mature divinity depicted in other Roman paintings.[5]

The painting is executed on a thin, narrow panel of wood 182 mm high and 47 mm wide at its greatest width, with a thickness varying from 1.5 to 2.5 mm. There are finished straight edges at the top and bottom and along most of the left-hand side, but not at the right, where the picture seems incomplete and the edge is at first straight but then indents, leaving an irregular lacuna where a piece of wood has evidently broken away. The panel is not flat but slightly distorted, more noticeably at the top, where the painted surface is somewhat convex. Some of the surface of the wood has been lost, particularly along the top edge and at the upper left corner, and there are three deeper cavities, seemingly chiselled or gouged out, one at the left side and two at the right. The back of the panel is plain and

shows a notable compression of the wood at the top and bottom to a depth of 4 and 3 mm respectively, suggesting that it was originally gripped in a frame. This is echoed on the painted surface by areas of intact but bare wood along the upper edge, about 2 mm deep, and a thickening of the paint towards the left-hand side, resulting in a whitish line running parallel to the edge in the upper part.

The surface of the painting is discoloured and there are deposits obscuring the details in some places; small areas of paint have been lost and the colours are faded. There is no evidence of an extensive preparatory ground of plaster or gesso applied to the wood; rather, the painting seems to have been executed in tempera on a thin layer of wash similar to that found on writing boards. This shows as a white undercoat in places where the paint is missing.

Against a blue background, the goddess is shown wearing a golden disk-and-horns crown (the basileion), painted in red and yellow, with a rearing cobra on the front of the rather ovoid disk, and flanking golden sprays of corn at the base. The whole device rests on a gold diadem, shown as parallel bands of dark red then yellow, and behind this appears a mass of lighter red which is probably a floral wreath – the outline is scalloped, though no internal indications of petals or flowers are apparent. Below the diadem, the goddess' hair is arranged in a neat formation of tight curls which descend over her forehead, with a looser fall of long curling locks onto her shoulders on either side. Her pale-pink face, shown slightly three-quarters to the left, is long and serious, with emphatically large eyes and curving eyebrows shown in black. The expressiveness of the eyes is intensified by the apparent highlighting of the whites, but this is in fact due to the loss of paint here, as elsewhere on the face. Her narrow, shapely nose is sketched in red, and she has a small mouth with full pink lips outlined in red, strokes of which also shade her left cheek. Around the goddess' neck is the reddish line of a necklace with traces of yellow at the left suggesting that it was originally depicted as gold; from it hangs a dark, indistinct pendant. She also wears pendent earrings of a reversed-s shape, indicated in faint whitish-yellow lines. Below the pendant of her necklace are the folds of a tunic, shown in brownish-red, over which is a yellow mantle knotted over her right breast.[6] Details of her dress, at her left side are unclear and mostly lost in the break; she may have worn a floral garland draped diagonally over her left shoulder, as shown on other representations of Isis.

Iconographically there are many three-dimensional

---

[5] The painting has previously been published by C. A. Hope, 'Isis and Serapis at Kellis: a brief note', *Bulletin of the Australian Centre for Egyptology* 5 (1994), 37–42. I am grateful to Dr Hope for the opportunity to provide a longer discussion here, and to Michelle Berry for discussing the technical aspects of the panel with me.

[6] The complexities of this costume, apparently composed of three items of dress (tunic, robe and shawl), not two, have been discussed by R. S. Bianchi, 'Not the Isis Knot', *Bulletin of the Egyptological Seminar* 2 (1980), 9–31, who takes classical archaeologists to task for misinterpreting the ensemble. However, the accuracy of its depiction in Graeco-Roman works is open to question.

representations of Isis of Hellenistic and Roman date with which to compare the goddess on the Kellis panel (Eingartner 1991), and the category of terracotta figures in particular may provide parallels which are of relevance for the religious context as well as the style of depiction (Dunand 1979, 60–70 and *passim*).[7] There are few painted examples, however; the most closely comparable is that belonging to the set of painted wooden triptych panels in the Getty Museum, where a central commemorative portrait of a màn is flanked by busts of Isis and Serapis on the hinged folding wings, which are stylistically rather different to the central panel (Thompson 1978–9, 185–92; 1982, 24, 46–51, 66 no. 8).[8] The Getty picture presents a more mature image of Isis, executed in a fluid and vigorous technique which contrasts with the delicacy of the Kellis portrait, a contrast which is heightened by its much better state of preservation. The style and colouring of the painting are heavier. The goddess' tunic is blue, the fringed mantle over it a pinkish-brown with yellow highlights and red folds, and a pink floral garland falls diagonally from her left shoulder; there is no fringe apparent on the yellow mantle in the Kellis picture. The gaze of the Getty Isis seems distant, turned to her left and slightly upwards, where Isis of Kellis looks out at the spectator with a sober directness.[9]

The details of the portrayal answer to those of the Kellis image but they are not closely similar. The goddess' hair falls in looser wavy locks to her shoulders from a more natural central parting. She wears two necklaces and s-curved dolphin pendent earrings; around her head behind her headdress is a wreath of pink flowers and curving green leaves. The headdress itself (disk, horns and flanking sprigs) seems to support a light-coloured veil which descends to her shoulders.[10]

Similar details appear on an Isiac portrait formerly in the Maurice Nahman collection in Cairo (Eingartner 1991, 169–70 no. 145, Plate 90). As the wooden panel on which it was painted seems to have been cut down for reuse as a mummy portrait, it would seem that the subject was a priestess or worshipper of Isis rather than the goddess herself. It is significant that she has no headdress, although the curlicues radiating around the periphery of her hair may indicate a floral wreath rather than loose curls; she holds a sistrum in her right hand but a small floral garland, as often shown on mummy portraits, in her left. From her left shoulder a floral-patterned stole, rather than a garland, falls to cross diagonally over her knotted shawl. She wears pearl-drop earrings and a chain necklace with a pendant, more elaborate jewels than are shown in the Kellis painting, but her hairstyle is comparable – tight curls extending over the top of the head onto the forehead, with bunched locks falling onto her shoulders. The similarity of the upper part of her hairstyle to the rich bank of curls surmounting the head which was fashionable in Roman women's hairdressing of the Flavian period has led Parlasca (1977, 48 no. 82, Plate 20.1) to suggest a late first century date for this painting, although he notes that the lower 'Isis locks' would not be consistent with this fashion.[11] The point is significant, since the curls shown both on this portrait and the Kellis example are not exactly like the Flavian style but might be compared with the serried corkscrew curls falling over the forehead, typified by the hairstyle of the New York statuette of the deified Arsinoe II, where the drilling of the ends of the curls over the brow emphasizes their tightness.[12] This more authentically Egyptian manner of dressing the hair over the top of the head, reminiscent of the elaborate tight curls of pharaonic wigs, is less frequently encountered than the more naturalistic style with waves falling from a central parting, as shown on the Getty portrait.[13]

It has been suggested that the portraits of Isis and Serapis on the Getty triptych may be derived from celebrated paintings, perhaps cult images in Alexandria (Thompson [quoting J. Frel] 1978–9, 190; 1982, 48). Even the modest range of comparison offered here, however, with the Kellis panel and the Nahman mummy

---

[7] Most of the terracotta representations have been dated to the second and third centuries CE.

[8] Thompson suggested a date in the mid-third century on the basis of the central portrait; Parlasca (1977, 69 no. 405), prefers a late Antonine dating, (second half of the second century), followed by M. Nowicka, *Le portrait dans la peinture antique*, Warsaw, 1993, 172 and fig. 65. Most recently, a dating to the last two decades of the second century has been proposed in S. Walker, M. Bierbrier et al., *Ancient Faces. Mummy Portraits from Roman Egypt*, London, 1997, 123–4 no. 119, where the stylistic difference between the wings and the central portrait is noted.

[9] The correct position of the wings of the Getty triptych is unknown; Thompson (1978–9, 190–1) suggests that the Isis and Serapis portraits were hung with the painted surface facing inwards, so that they could be seen when the triptych was open and would thus meet the viewer's gaze, since the open wings would be at an angle. However, the eyes of both divinities are directed upwards by comparison with those of the man in the central portrait, who does look directly at the viewer. The triptych panels are unprovenanced but presumed to have been made for a domestic shrine.

[10] There are no traces of such a feature on the Kellis portrait – a straight white line passing between the horns of the headdress is seemingly the result of surface damage.

[11] For a convenient list of mummy portraits with Isiac features, see Eingartner 1991, 83–5, and the more recent discussion by B. Borg, *Mummienporträts. Chronologie und kultureller Kontext*, Mainz, 1996, 112–21.

[12] MMA 20.2.21; B. V. Bothmer, *Egyptian Sculpture of the Late Period*, Brooklyn, 1961, 159–60 no. 123, Figures 307–10; more recently, R. S. Bianchi in R. S. Bianchi et al., *Cleopatra's Egypt*, Brooklyn, 1988, 170–2 no. 66, and cf. 182 no. 74.

[13] See Dunand's (1979, 24–5) discussion of the type and dating of hairstyles represented on terracotta figures of Isis.

Plate 3 Painted panel of Isis (registration no. 31/420–D6–1/D/1/152).

portrait, demonstrates that although there is a generic similarity between these figures, by the Roman Period there was a variety of iconography which takes us far from any single famous painted original.

The Kellis portrait is a significant addition to the small corpus of panel paintings, other than mummy portraits, which have survived from Roman Egypt. Even rarer are those which have come from an archaeological context. In a house excavated in Tebtunis early in this century, many fragments of painted panels were found on the floor of a room where they had fallen from the walls: it was possible to reconstruct one, complete with its frame – a picture of Suchos and Isis enthroned, with a small figure of Harpocrates standing between them (Rubensohn 1905, 16–25, Plate 1; Parlasca 1966, 69 note 66).[14] These were evidently private devotional images, truly 'icons', in our sense of the word, as their excavator Otto Rubensohn (1905, 22) noted.[15] Other surviving examples, of which the provenance is unknown, demonstrate by their subject matter and style that they too belong to this category of domestic images, in which the subjects are often obscure, even unidentifiable, deities, and the level of artistic skill is variable.[16] Such panels have been generally ascribed to the Fayum, on the basis of the few provenanced examples, and also because of their good state of preservation and their relationship to the mummy portraits on panels. The new example from Kellis shows that, as with the mummy portraits, we should expect their occurrence in other parts of Egypt as well.

While it most likely belongs to this category of private devotional image, the find-spot of the panel suggests that it may have served as a votive object, perhaps after a period of domestic use. The physical evidence indicates that it was once framed, but whether it was a single painting or part of a folding triptych we cannot tell; it seems too thin to have served the latter purpose, even with the protection of a surrounding frame.[17] Such panel paintings were customarily made of several narrow strips of wood laid side by side;[18] the survival of incomplete pictures on single strips testifies to the vulnerability of this kind of assemblage.[19] The depiction of Isis in the Kellis painting may have been completed on a second strip of wood laid to the right (hence the straight edge along the upper part here), with the possibility of further strips to the right showing one or more other figures. The panel is quite short by comparison with other examples, which fall within a general range of 40 to 65 cm in height,[20] but it seems too tall and thin to have served as a box panel.[21] A small single picture, perhaps with a flanking bust of Serapis, seems likely to have been its original form.

Most of the surviving panels have been dated to the second or third centuries CE on stylistic grounds, with little other evidence to confirm this. The context in which the Kellis picture was found does not provide secure dating evidence for it, and if it was indeed a votive offering, it may have been in the temple for some time before the building ceased to be used as a place of worship in the fourth century, and possibly in a private house for some time even before that. A dating in the second century CE may not be improbable, given the refined style of the painting and also the pronounced Egyptian aspects of the portrayal in hairstyle and dress – the figure seems to hark back to the imagery of Ptolemaic depictions of Isis, or queens with Isiac attributes, rather than resembling the fulsome female divinities and personifications of later Roman art.

[14] The painting illustrated by Rubensohn, Berlin 15978, was subsequently destroyed; the type of frame is discussed by Ehlich (1954, 80–2). Rubensohn's Plate 2 shows another fragmentary panel from the same room, depicting Athena.

[15] On the basis of papyri found here and in the adjoining rooms he proposed a date in the second–early third century for the paintings.

[16] M. Rostovtzeff's survey is old but still useful and illustrates several panels which are now lost: 'Kleinasiatische und syrische Götter in römischen Ägypten', *Aegyptus* 13 (1933), 493–513. See also D. L. Thompson, 'The Hartford Horseman', *Chronique d'Égypte* 50 (1975), 321–5; Friedman 1989, 188–9 no. 98.

[17] For the permutations of triptych frames, see Ehlich 1954, 177 fig. 49 (reprised by Thompson 1978-9, 191, and 1982, 50); simple frames for single pictures are discussed by Ehlich 1954, 80–93.

[18] See, for instance, Rubensohn 1905, Plate 1 which was made of five strips of wood; and the Heron panel in Rhode Island, also consisting of five strips (Friedman 1989, 188–9).

[19] See for instance the incomplete divinities of Louvre P207 and Cairo J. 87191: Parlasca 1966, 60 and Plate 21.1 and 3.

[20] The wings of the Getty triptych are 40 cm high; the tallest of the examples listed by Rostovtzeff (496–7 and Figure 5, see note 16 above) is just over 65 cm (the lost MacGregor panel showing a seated Isis and two young men). Of exceptional height (76.1 cm) are the two hinged panels in Berkeley depicting military gods: Thompson 1978-9, 189–91, Figures 5–6.

[21] Cf. the two painted box panels from the Faiyum showing full-length figures of Isis and Aphrodite on a red ground: British Museum GR 1902.9–17, 1 (10.5 by 4.7 by 0.21 cm, max. ht. by w. by thickness) and 2 (10.1 by 7.1 by 0.2 cm; warped), dated to the second half of the third century CE: R. P. Hinks, *Catologue of the Greek, Etruscan and Roman Paintings and Mosaics in the British Museum,* London, 1933, 59–61 nos 89–90 (dating them to the fourth century). For further details of these I am indebted to Donald Bailey.

Bibliography

Allberry, C. R. C., 1938 *Manichaean Manuscripts in the Chester Beatty Collection. Volume II: A Manichaean Psalm-Book, Part II*, Stuttgart.

Auth, S., 1991 'Coptic Glass', in *The Coptic Encyclopedia*, Volume 4, ed. A. S. Attiya, New York, 1143–47.

Bagnall, R. S., 1997 *The Kellis Agricultural Account Book*, Oxford.

Bagnall, R. S., U. Thanheiser and K. A. Worp, 1998 'Tiphagion', *Zeitschrift für Papyrologie und Epigraphik* 122, 173–81.

Bailey, D., 1990 'Classical Architecture in Roman Egypt', in *Architecture and Architectural Sculpture in the Roman Empire*, ed. M. Henig, Oxford, 121–37.

Ballet, P., 1990 'La céramique di site urbain de Douch/Kysis', *Bulletin de L'Institut Français d'Archéologie Orientale* 90, 298–301.

Barakat, H., 1990 'Plant Remains from el Omari', in F. Debono and B. Mortensen, *El Omari. A Neolithic Settlement and other Sites in the Vicinity of Wadi Hof, Helwan*, Mainz am Rhein, 109–14.

Beadnell, H., 1901 *Dakhleh Oasis: Its Topography and Geology*, Cairo.

Bowen, G. E., C. A. Hope and O. E. Kaper, 1993 'A Brief Report on the Excavations at Ismant el-Kharab in 1992–93', *Bulletin of the Australian Centre for Egyptology* 4, 17–28.

Brogan, O. and D. J. Smith, 1984 *Ghirza. A Libyan settlement in the Roman Period*, Tripoli.

Caton-Thompson, G., 1952 *Kharga Oasis in Prehistory*, London.

Caton-Thompson, G. and E. W. Gardner, 1934 *The Desert Fayum*, London.

Cauville, S., 1990 *Le temple de Dendera: guide archéologique*, Cairo.

Charlesworth, D., 1966 'Roman square Bottles', *Journal of Glass Studies* 8, 20–40.

Collis, J., 1988 'Data for Dating', in *Coins and the Archaeologist*, eds J. Casey and R. Reece, London, 189–99.

Coulon, L., F. Leclère and S. Marchand, 1995 '<<Catacombes>> Osiriennes de Ptolémée IV à Karnak: Rapport préliminaire de la campagne de fouilles 1993', *Cahiers de Karnak* X, 205–8.

Crowfoot, E., 1979 'Textiles', in R. D. Anderson and W. Y. Adams, 'Qasr Ibrim 1978', *Journal of Egyptian Archaeology* 65, 39–40.

Debono, F., 1948 'el-Omari (près d'Helouan)', *Annales du Service des Antiquités Égyptiennes* 48, 561–9.

Dunand F., 1979 *Religion populaire en Égypte romaine*, Leiden.

Ehlich, W., 1954 *Bild und Rahmen im Altertum*, Munich.

Eingartner, J., 1991 *Isis und ihre Dienerinnen in der Kunst der römische Kaiserzeit*, Leiden.

Fakhry, A., 1951 *The Necropolis of el-Bagawat in Kharga Oasis*, Cairo.

Flannery, K.V., 1972 'The origins of the village as a settlement type in Mesoamerica and the 'Near East: a comparative study', in *Man, Settlement and Urbanism*, eds P. J. Ucko, R. Tringham and G. W. Dimbleby, London, 23–53.

de Franciscis, A., 1963 'Vetri Antichi Scoperti ad Ercolana', *Journal of Glass Studies* 5, 137–42.

Frey, R., 1986 'Dakhleh Oasis Project: Interim Report on Excavations at the 'Ein Tirghi Cemetery', *Journal of the Society for the Study of Egyptian Antiquities* XVI, 92–102.

Friedman, F. D., 1989 *Beyond the Pharaohs. Egypt and the Copts in the 2nd to 7th Centuries. A. D.*, Rhode Island.

Gardner, I., 1993 'A Manichaean Liturgical Codex found at Kellis', *Orientalia* 62, 30–59.

Gardner, I., 1997 'Personal Letters from the Manichaean Community at Kellis', in *Atti del Terzo Congresso Internazionale di Studi "Manicheismo e Oriente Christiano Antico"*, eds L. Curillo and A. van Tongerloo, Louvain / Naples, 77–94.

Gautier, G., 1981 'Monnaies trouveé à Douche', *Bulletin de L'Institut Français d'Archéologie Orientale* 81, 111–14.

Germer, R., 1985 *Flora des pharaonischen Ägypten*, Mainz am Rhein.

Gilman, P. A., 1987 'Architecture as artifact: pit structures and pueblos in American Southwest', *American Antiquity* 52, 538–64.

Giversen, S., 1988 *The Manichaean Coptic Papyri in the Chester Beatty Library, Volumes III and IV*, Geneva.

Handler, S., 1971 'Architecture on the Roman Coins of Alexandria', *American Journal of Archaeology* 75, 57–74.

Harden, D. B., 1936 *Roman Glass from Karanis*, Michigan.

Hassan, F. A., 1988 'The Predynastic of Egypt', *Journal of World Prehistory* 2, 135–85.

Hayes, J. W., 1975 *Roman and Pre-Roman Glass in the Royal Ontario Museum*, Toronto.

Helbaek, H., 1953 'Queen Icheti's Wheat', *Koneglige Danske Videnskabernes Selskab Biologiske Meddelelser* 21.8, 3–17.

Hobler, P. M. and J. J. Hester, 1969 *Prehistoric Settlement Patterns in the Libyan Desert*, Salt Lake City.

Hope, C. A., 1979 'Dakhleh Oasis Project: Report on the Study of the Pottery and Kilns', *Journal of the Society for the Study of Egyptian Antiquities* IX, 187–201.

Hope, C. A., 1980 'Dakhleh Oasis Project: Report on the Study of the Pottery and Kilns', *Journal of the Society for the Study of Egyptian Antiquities* X, 283–313.

Hope, C. A., 1981 'Dakhleh Oasis Project: Report on the Study of the Pottery and Kilns: Third Season – 1980',

Journal of the Society for the Study of Egyptian Antiquities
XI, 233–41.

Hope, C. A., 1985 'Dakhleh Oasis Project: Report on the 1986 Excavations at Ismant el-Gharab', *Journal of the Society for the Study of Egyptian Antiquities* XV, 114–25.

Hope, C. A., 1986 'Dakhleh Oasis Project: Report on the 1987 Excavations at Ismant el-Gharab', *Journal of the Society for the Study of Egyptian Antiquities* XVI, 74–91.

Hope, C. A., 1987 'The Dakhleh Oasis Project: Ismant el-Kharab 1988–1990', *Journal of the Society for the Study of Egyptian Antiquities* XVII, 157–76.

Hope, C. A., 1988 'Three Seasons of Excavation at Ismant el-Gharab in Dakhleh Oasis, Egypt', *Mediterranean Archaeology* I, 160–78.

Hope, C. A., 1990 'Excavations at Ismant el-Kharab in the Dakhleh Oasis', *Journal of the Society for the Study of Egyptian Antiquities* 1, 43–54.

Hope, C. A., 1991 'The 1991 Excavations at Ismant el-Kharab in the Dakhleh Oasis', *Journal of the Society for the Study of Egyptian Antiquities* 2, 41–50.

Hope, C. A., 1998 'Early Pottery from the Dakhleh Oasis', *Bulletin of the Australian Centre for Egyptology* 9, 53–60.

Hope, C. A., in press a 'Observations on the Dating of the Occupation at Ismant el-Kharab' in *The Oasis Papers: Proceedings of the First International Symposium of the Dakhleh Oasis Project*, ed. C. A. Marlow, Oxford.

Hope, C. A., in press b 'Pottery Manufacture in the Dakhleh Oasis', in *Reports from the Survey of Dakhleh Oasis, Western Desert of Egypt, 1977–1987*, eds C. S. Churcher and A. J. Mills, Oxford.

Hope, C. A., O. E. Kaper and G. Bowen, 1992 'Excavations at Ismant el-Kharab – 1992', *Bulletin of the Australian Centre for Egyptology* 3, 41–9.

Hope, C. A., O. E. Kaper, G. E. Bowen and S. F. Patten, 1989 'Dakhleh Oasis Project: Ismant el-Kharab 1991–92', *Journal of the Society for the Study of Egyptian Antiquities* 19, 1–26.

Kaper, O. E., 1991 'The God Tutu (Tithoes) and his Temple in the Dakhleh Oasis', *Bulletin of the Australian Centre for Egyptology* 2, 59–67.

Kaper, O. E., 1997 'A painting of the Gods of Dakhleh in the Temple of Tutu', in *The Temple in Ancient Egypt*, ed. S. Quirke, London, 204–15.

Kaper, O. E. and K. A. Worp, 1995 'A Bronze Representing Tapsais of Kellis', *Revue d'Égyptologie* 46, 107–18.

Kees, H., 1955 *Das Alte Ägypten*, Berlin.

Keimer, L., 1924 *Die Gartenpflanzen im Alten Ägypten*, Hildesheim.

Kent, J. P. C., 1981 *Roman Imperial Coinage, Volume VIII*, London.

Knudstad, J. E. and R. A. Frey, in press 'Ismant el-Kharab: Survey at a Roman Town', in *Reports from the Survey of Dakhleh Oasis, Western Desert of Egypt 1977–1987*, eds C. S. Churcher and A. J. Mills, Oxford.

Lucas, A., 1962 *Ancient Egyptian Materials and Industries* (4th edn, revised by J. R. Harris), London.

Lyttleton, M., 1974 *Baroque Architecture in Classical Antiquity*, London.

McDonald, M. M. A., 1990a. 'Dakhleh Oasis Project. Holocene Prehistory: Interim Report on the 1988 and 1989 Seasons', *Journal of the Society for the Study of Egyptian Antiquities* XX, 24–53.

McDonald, M. M. A., 1990b 'Dakhleh Oasis Project. Holocene

Prehistory: interim report on the 1990 season', *Journal of the Society for the Study of Egyptian Antiquities* XX, 54–64.

McDonald, M. M. A., 1990c 'Dakhleh Oasis Project. Holocene Prehistory: interim report on the 1991 season', *Journal of the Society for the Study of Egyptian Antiquities* XX, 65–76.

McDonald, M. M. A., 1991 'Technological organization and sedentism in the Epipalaeolithic of Dakhleh Oasis, Egypt', *African Archaeological Review* 9, 81–109.

McKenzie, J., 1990 *The Architecture of Petra*, Oxford.

Mills, A. J., 1982 'The Dakhleh Oasis Project. Report on the Fourth Season of the Survey October 1981–January 1982', *Journal of the Society for the Study of Egyptian Antiquities* XII, 93–101.

Mills, A. J., 1983 'The Dakhleh Oasis Project. Report on the Fifth Season of Survey October, 1982–January, 1983', *Journal of the Society for the Study of Egyptian Antiquities* XIII, 121–41.

Mills, A. J., 1984 'The Dakhleh Oasis Project. Report on the Sixth Season of Survey: 1983–1984', *Journal of the Society for the Study of Egyptian Antiquities* XIV, 81–5.

Mills, A. J., 1990a 'The Dakhleh Oasis Project. Report on the 1990–1991 Field Season', *Journal of the Society for the Study of Egyptian Antiquities* XX, 11–16.

Mills, A. J., 1990b 'Dakhleh Oasis Project. Report on the 1991–1992 Field Season', *Journal of the Society for the Study of Egyptian Antiquities* XX, 17–23.

Milne, J. B., 1971 *The Catalogue of Alexandrian Coins*, Oxford.

Neumann, K., 1989 'Zur Vegetationsgeschichte der Ostsahara im Holazän. Holzkohlen aus prähistorischen Fundstellen', in *Forschungen zur Umweltgeschichte der Ostsahara*, ed. R. Kuper, Köln, 13–181.

Osing, J., 1982 'Das Grab des Qtjjnws', in J. Osing et al., *Denkmäler der Oase Dachla*, Mainz am Rhein, 58–69.

Patten, S. F., 1993 'Dakhleh Oasis Project, 1992', *Bulletin de Liaison du Groupe International d'Étude de la Céramique Égyptienne* XVII, 37–40.

Patten, S. F., 1996 'Dakhleh Oasis Project 1994 Season', *Bulletin de Liaison du Groupe International d'Étude de la Céramique Égyptienne* XIX, 51–5.

Parlasca, K., 1966 *Mummienporträts und verwandte Denkmäler*, Wiesbaden.

Parlasca, K., 1977 *Ritratti di Mummie. Repertorio d'arte dell'Egitto greco-romano* ser. B, II, Rome.

Percival, J., 1974 *The Wheat Plant*, London.

Poole, R. J., 1892 *Catalogue of the Coins of Alexandria and the Nomes*, London.

Price, M. and B. Trell., 1977 *Coins and their Cities*, London.

Quaegebeur, J., 1993 'L'autel-à-feu et l'abattoir en Égypte tardive', in *Ritual and Sacrifice in the Ancient Near East*, ed. J. Quaegebeur, Leuven, 329–53.

Reddé, M., 1990 'Quinze années de recherches française à Douch: vers un premier bilan', *Bulletin de L'Institut Français d'Archéologie Orientale* 90, 281–93.

Ritchie, J., in press 'Flora, Vegetation and Palaeobotany', in *Reports from the Survey of Dakhleh Oasis, Western Desert of Egypt, 1977–1987*, eds C. S. Churcher and A. J. Mills, Oxford.

Rubensohn, O., 1905 'Aus griechisch-römischen Häusern des Fayum', *Jahrbuch des deutschen Archäologischen Instituts* 20, 1–25.

el-Sayed, R., 1982 *La déese Neith de Saïs*, Cairo.

Schäfer, H., 1986 *Principles of Egyptian Art* (ed. by E. Brunner-Traut, and ed. and translated by J. Baines), Oxford.

Schiemann, E., 1954 'Einkorn im Alten Ägypten', *Der Züchter* 24, 139–49.

Schweinfurth, 1887 'Die letzten botanischen Entdeckungen in den Gräbern Ägyptens', *Botanische Jahrbücher* 8, 1–16.

Smith, A. B., 1992 *Pastoralism in Africa: origins and development ecology*, Athens (Ohio).

Täckholm, V., 1951 'Botantical Identification', in J-P. Lauer, V. Laurent-Täckholm and Åberg, *Les plantes découvertes dans les souterrains de l'enceinte du roi Zoser à Saqqarah (IIIe Dynastie)*, Cairo, 121–52.

Täckholm, V. and M. Drar, 1950 *Flora of Egypt II*, Cairo.

Täckholm, V. and G. Täckholm, 1941 *Flora of Egypt I*, Cairo.

Tatton-Brown, V., 1991 'The Roman Empire', in *Five Thousand Years of Glass*, ed. H. Tait, London, 62–97.

Thanheiser, U., in press 'Über den Ackerbau in dynasticher Zeit. Ergebnisse der Untersuchung von Pflanzenresten aue tell el-Dab'a', in M. Bietak, J. Dorner, J. Boessneck, A. van den Driesch, H. Egger and U. Thanheiser, *Tell el-Dab'a VIII*, Vienna.

Thompson, D. L., 1978–9 'A painted triptych from Roman Egypt', *J. Paul Getty Museum Journal* 6–7, 185–92.

Thompson, D. L., 1982 *Mummy Portraits in the J. Paul Getty Museum* (rev. edn), Malibu, 1982.

Wagner, G., 1973 'Inscriptions grecques des oasis de Dakhleh et Bahriyeh découvertes par le Dr. Ahmed Fakhry', *Bulletin de L'Institut Français d'Archéologie Orientale* 73, 177–92.

Wagner, G., 1990 'τιφαγιον', *Zeitschrift für Papyrologie und Epigraphik* 80, 239–41.

Wallert, I., 1962 *Die Palmen im Alten Ägypten*, Munich.

Wendorf, F., A. E. Close, R. Schild, K. Wasylikowa, R. A. Housley, J. R. Harlan and H. Królik 1992 'Saharan exploitation of plants 8,000 years bp', *Nature* 359, 721–724.

Winlock, H. E., 1936 *Ed Dakhleh Oasis*, New York.

Worp, K. A., 1995 *Greek Papyri from Kellis I*, Oxford.

van Zeist, W., 1983 'A Palaeobotanical Study of Neolithic Erbaba, Turkey', *Anatolica* 10, 47–89.

Zohary, D. and Hopf., 1988 *Domestication of Plants in the Old World*, Oxford.